此登攀
SCALE THE HEIGHTS

陈家泠天马行空艺术人生
Master Chen Jialing's Dramatic Art Life

许根顺 摄影 撰文
Photos & Words by Xu Genshun

上海大学出版社
Shanghai University Press

目 录
Contents

6 / Preface
序言 / 7

Prologue: A half-century's partnership between
Xu Genshun and his teacher Chen Jialing
楔 子　亦师亦友 50 年
——许根顺与他的老师陈家泠 / 13

1 17 / Shanghai University's Centennial Legacy
百年上大 / 17

2 29 / Sacred Places' Revolutionary Heritage
红色圣地 / 29

3 109 / China's Magnificent Landscape
壮丽祖国 / 109

4 199 / A World of Harmony and Beauty
和美世界 / 199

5 285 / Artistic Creation
艺术创作 / 285

334 / Epilogue
后记 / 335

Preface

Red flags stream in the wind in a blaze of glory.

This year marks the 75th anniversary of the founding of the People's Republic of China, and the 10th anniversary of the publication of *Speech at the Forum of Art and Literature* by General Secretary Xi Jinping. *Scale the Heights: Master Chen Jialing's Dramatic Art Life* photographed and compiled by Photographer Xu Genshun is not only a precious gift for the birthday of the Republic, but also a vivid record documenting the efforts to implement the tenets of Xi Jinping's speech.

Co-founded in 1922 by the Communist Party of China (CPC) and the Kuomintang (KMT) during the early period of the two parties' cooperation, Shanghai University was the first accredited university under de facto leadership of CPC. For the past 100-odd years, the university has been fully committed to the education and cultivation of outstanding talents. From the early objectives of "cultivating national leaders and promoting cultural undertakings" to the current mission of "cultivating talents to benefit the country and mankind and promoting the progress of social civilization", it has passed down its revolutionary legacy and nurtured batches of talents who are full of national spirit and social responsibility. A typical case is Prof. Chen Jialing.

Mr. Chen Jialing from Shanghai Academy of Fine Arts, Shanghai University is a leading figure of contemporary new Shanghai style art. Since 1970s and 80s, he has explored assiduously Chinese painting with its unique features and kept updated. His artistic trajectories and outstanding achievements in the field of Chinese painting have become an index for people both at home and abroad to appreciate the latest changes in art locally and nationally. As an exemplary SHUer, he has forged his firm beliefs and convictions through his artistic career as well as through his profound understanding of the history of CPC.

These firm convictions have ignited a powerful life force in the heart of Chen Jialing, an artist in his late eighties. Cherishing the high aspiration

序言

风展红旗如画。

今年是中华人民共和国成立75周年,也是习近平总书记《在文艺工作座谈会上的讲话》发表10周年。由摄影家许根顺摄影、撰文的《肯登攀——陈家泠天马行空艺术人生》一书既是献给共和国华诞的一份珍贵礼物,也是努力贯彻习近平总书记《在文艺工作座谈会上的讲话》的一份记录生动的影像文献。

成立于1922年的上海大学,是国共两党携手合作、由中国共产党实际领导的第一所正规大学。百余年来,学校行育人之大道,以水滴石穿的执着,启智润心的情怀化成天下,培育英才。从建校之初"养成建国人才,促进文化事业"的办学宗旨到当下"养成强国济世人才,促进社会文明进步"的使命,学校赓续红色血脉,培育了一批批饱含家国情怀和社会担当的国之英才,陈家泠教授就是其中的典型代表。

陈家泠先生是当代新海派美术的领军人物。从20世纪七八十年代,他就开始孜孜不倦,与时俱进地探索独具特色的中国画艺术。他的艺术道路,他在中国画领域所取得的卓越成就,已经成为海内外了解上海和中国美术最新变化的索引。作为上人,他以他的艺术生涯,以他对中国共产党历史深刻的理解,铸就自己坚定的信仰和信念。

of "visiting all places of interest before I get old", he trudged across mountains and waded through rivers despite his advanced age, leaving footprints in the grass huts of Shaoshan, on the peak of Jinggang Mountain, up the steep stonesteps of Loushan Pass, under the trees in the Jujube Garden of Yan'an, in front of the impregnable bulwark of Taihang Mountain, and inside the cave dwellings of Xibaipo. He has visited the scenes of Chinese Revolution one by one to feel in person the solemnity and passion of history. He has created on the rice paper great portraits of the Revolutionary Shrines which are characteristic of a contemporary artist and full of the flavor of the times, showcasing the spiritual genealogy passed down by the Chinese communists behind the portraits. To commemorate the centennial anniversary of CPC, he presents to the faculty and students of Shanghai University "Red Star Shines over Me" — painting and calligraphy exhibition of revolutionary sites, and "Ode to the Plum Blossom" — painting and calligraphy exhibition, to depict the national spirit.

Prof. Xu Genshun from Studio of Public Diplomacy and Urban Culture, School of Continuing Education, Shanghai University is Mr. Chen Jialing's early student. A famed photographer as well, he has photographed more than 800 heads of state, heads of government and first ladies around the world coming to visit Shanghai, which has left precious historical documents for China's public diplomacy and reform and opening up. For the last two decades, he has followed Mr. Chen Jialing closely, recording with his camera the tracks of Master Chen devoted to his calling. The collection of pictures is an embodiment of a daunting spirit and a willing heart to scale the heights. The one hundred or so splendid pictures are all taken from "Scale the Heights" — Xu Genshun's Photography Exhibition grandly opened at the centennial anniversary of Shanghai University. These splendid pictures, either in macroscopic or microscopic perspectives, reveal to the viewers Master Chen Jialing's artistic spirit of simplicity, elegance, flexibility

强烈的信念,在年近九旬的艺术家内心燃起了强大的生命力量。

他以"踏遍青山人未老"的凌云壮志,耄耋之年不畏艰难险阻,爬山涉水,走进韶山冲的草屋,眺望井冈山的雄姿,攀援娄山关险峻的石阶,留恋在延河之滨的枣园树下,伫立在太行山的铜墙铁壁,留恋在西柏坡窑洞前的沉思……一瞻临中国革命的现场,在现场感受历史曾经的悲壮和激情。他披星戴月,不舍昼夜,尽情地用笔墨色彩,在宣纸上留下了当代艺术家充满时代气息的革命圣地的伟大肖像,以及蕴藏在肖像背后中国共产党人代代相传的精神谱系,在中国共产党建党 100 年华诞之际,向上海大学师生献上了"红星照我行"——红色革命圣地书画展和书写民族精神的"咏梅"书画展。

上海大学继续教育学院"公共外交与城市文化工作室"的许根顺教授,是陈家泠先生早年的学生,也是知名摄影家,他先后为来沪的全球 800 多位国家元首、政府首脑、第一夫人留影,为中国公共外交和改革开放留下了珍贵的历史文献。近 20 多年来,他形影不离地追随陈家泠先生,以镜头记录了陈家泠"世上无难事,只要肯登攀",向着艺术高峰攀援的历程。本书的100 多件作品选自上海大学建校百年之际隆重开幕的许根顺"肯登攀"摄影展。这些作品既气势磅礴,又精细入微地留下了陈家泠先生"正入万山圈子里,一山放过一山拦",展现了

and innovation. Just as a Tang poem depicts, "You are surrounded by ten thousand mountains high/One mountain lets you pass, another bars your way", they narrate vividly to the audience the single-minded, head-on artistic pursuit of Master Chen as a martyr to his lifelong cause.

Each photo shares with us an inspiring story of Chen Jialing, a SHUer and an art legend. Each photo also tells the story of Xu Genshun, an unsung hero behind the scenes. Without this long-suffering partner and prolific co-creator, Master Chen wouldn't have accomplished what he set out to do. Each of the 100 or so photos bears witness to Xu's uncomplaining dedication.

"River and mountains like a painting/How many heroes passed them once". Although *Scale the Heights: Master Chen Jialing's Dramatic Art Life* highlights the master's art life, it is the joint efforts of these two SHUers who epitomize the very spirit of "striving constantly for self-improvement", the mission statement of Shanghai University. This is an exhibition, but more than an exhibition. Rather, it is a textbook of high artistic value co-authored by Master Chen and his student Xu Genshun, and a course integrating politics, culture, art and aesthetics taught by them.

Liu Changsheng
President of Shanghai University
Academician of Chinese Academy of Sciences
Aug. 28, 2024

其简极致美，灵变创新的艺术精神，义无反顾、一往无前的大师气质……

每张照片都讲述着上大人陈家泠励志的艺术传奇，也无言地留下了照片背后摄影家许根顺融融入式、沉浸式的忠诚坚持与无怨无悔的付出，是一种甘愿舍得奉献艺术的情怀。

"江山如画，一时多少豪杰"。《肯登攀——陈家泠天马行空艺术人生》以陈家泠艺术踪迹为主题内容，同时也是两个"上大人"的精神风采，全体上大人"自强不息"的真实写照，是陈家泠与许根顺师生共著的一部文化艺术内涵很高的教科书，更是一堂集政治、文化、艺术、美学一体的大课。

是为序。

刘昌胜
上海大学校长、中国科学院院士
2024年8月28日

Prologue

A half-century's
partnership between Xu Genshun
and his teacher Chen Jialing

I have been a student of Chen Jialing for at least 54 years (since 1970 when I attended Shanghai Fine Arts School). He is my most respected, trusted and loved teacher, a friend and a family member.

Master Chen often says that *An Ascent to Stork Hall* by Wang Zhihuan is a true depiction of his life. His current physical state is like "the setting sun" in the first line "The setting sun behind the mountains glows". His ideals and artistic achievements are like a river flowing into the sea as the second line "The muddy yellow river seawards flows" depicts. And the third line "If more distant views are what you desire, you simply climb up a story higher" is a kind of dialectics and relativity. Only by climbing steadfastly can one prolong the time the sun sets. Hence he cherishes the present and feels grateful for every moment of life.

Master Chen is a man of tenacity. He once walked all the way from Shanghai to Jinggang Mountain and Shaoshan. When he scaled a height, he would venture into every cave and explore every crack, and only felt his mission accomplished when reaching the peak. In 2014, he broke his femur while climbing to the top of a mountain for painting. On New Year's Day in 2015, when he just recovered, he set out again on the journey to Lotus Peak and Feilai Peak in Hangzhou, to collect painting materials of the West Lake for the coming G20 Summit.

Master Chen had painted a lot of porcelain works, but not many were fine works. In preparation for the second grand exhibition to be held in the National Museum of China, he spent a whole year in Jingdezhen, during which time he painted on 40 pieces of large vats (each weighing 1.5 tons with a diameter of 1.4 meter and a height of 1.5 meter). But only one-fifth were kept, of which 4 vats are collected by the National Museum of China. As he remarked, one piece of fine work is born out of countless pieces of craps.

楔 子

亦师亦友50年——许根顺与老师陈家泠

做陈家泠的学生,至今已54年(自1970年上海美术学校始),亦师亦友亦如家人,陈家泠是我尊敬、信任、亲近的老师。

陈家泠常常讲:王之涣的《登鹳雀楼》就是对他的真实写照,因为"白日依山尽"讲的是他现在的身体状态,太阳快要下山了;"黄河入海流"讲的是他的思想境界与艺术成就犹如小河汇入江河大海之中;"欲穷千里目,更上一层楼",是一种辩证法与相对论,只有不断攀登,才能够看到更长的太阳下山的时间,所以他尤为珍惜当下,感恩时代。

陈家泠身上有一股韧劲,他曾经从上海步行到井冈山、韶山。他登山时是见洞就钻、有缝必探,一定要攀登到山顶为止。2014年,因画画需高,他不幸摔断股骨。2015年新年第一天,伤情刚好,他就登上杭州的莲花峰、飞来峰,为创作G20西湖景色相关作品收集素材。

陈家泠画瓷很多,可精品却不多,为了中国国家博物馆第二次大展,他在景德镇待了整整一年,创作了40只大缸(每个缸重1.5吨,直径1.4米,高1.5米),最后仅保留了五分之一,其中4只缸被中国国家博物馆收为馆藏。他说:精品的背后是无数的废品。

Master Chen started to paint Chinese plums in response to CCTV's campaign to inspire the Winter Olympic athletes by the spirit of plum blossoms. It proved to be very effective. In fact, as early as 2014 and 2015, he went to Mount Lingshan and Mount Chaoshan in Hangzhou and Mount Tiantai in Zhejiang Province where he drew countless sketches of plum blossoms. During the Covid-19, he "kept himself indoors and thought behind closed doors"; he thought about the past, the present and the future. He spent 152 days poring over Chinese plum pieces from ancient to present times, and created 100 painting and calligraphy works of plum blossoms. The year 2022 marks the 100th anniversary of the founding of Shanghai University. On this special occasion, these plum blossoms radiate their distinctive beauty on the university campus. "April showers bring May flowers", this proverb is a crystallization of his life and a motto he wants to share with the faculty and students of Shanghai University.

For the past 20 or so years, I tracked and recorded every bit of my teacher's life, witnessing with my own eyes how his artistic development has evolved from "following the time to leading the time". In fact, photography is my second major. Over the past 40 years and more, I have left valuable historical materials for China's reform and development. In my database, there are numerous photos, videos and audio recordings of Chen Jialing. The huge database is a detailed account of my teacher's assiduous pursuit of art and artistic innovation.

I dedicate this to Prof. Chen Jialing, and to all the faculty and students of Shanghai University.

Xu Genshun
Spring, 2024

陈家泠画梅，缘于中央电视台的活动，用梅花精神来激励冬奥会运动员，效果很好。实际上，早在2014年，2015年，他就到了杭州灵山、超山，浙江天台山画了无数梅花的速写资料。2022年春，他"闭门思过"：思昨天、思今天、思明天，用了152天，从古到今，对梅花作了深入的研究，创作了100幅梅花书画作品。2022年恰逢上海大学建校百年，百幅梅花作品又有了在上大校园的梅花故事，"宝剑锋从磨砺出，梅花香自苦寒来"是他的人生写照，也是与上大师生的共勉。

我用了近20年时间，全程跟踪，记录了老师，亲历了他"绘画当随时代到引领时代"的艺术发展过程。其实摄影是我的第二专业，40多年来，我为中国改革发展留下了宝贵的历史资料。我的数据库里，有陈家泠的海量照片、视频和录音，巨大的数据库里都是老师对艺术的孜孜追求和对艺术创新的当代记录。

谨以此，献给陈家泠教授！献给上海大学全体师生！

许根顺

2024年春

百年上大

Shanghai University's Centennial Legacy

纪念上海大学建校100周年
THE 100TH ANNIVERSARY OF SHANGHAI UNIVERSITY

SINCE 1922

Some thoughts on rereading Mao Zedong's
*To the Tune of Prelude to the Melody of Water
Reascending Jinggang Mountain*

On the opening ceremony of "Scale the Heights" — the invited art exhibition of Chen Jialing to commemorate the centenary of Shanghai University, Chen Jialing gave a live recitation of Mao Zedong's *To the Tune of Prelude to the Melody of Water Reascending Jinggang Mountain* passionately, and presented the calligraphy work — Shanghai University's centennial legacy as a gift.

"吉登攀"——纪念上海大学建校100周年陈家泠艺术邀请特展开幕式场景
Scene of the opening ceremony of "Scale the Heights – the invited art exhibition of Chen Jialing" to commemorate the centenary of Shanghai University

重读毛泽东的《水调歌头·重上井冈山》有感

陈家泠在"吉登攀"——纪念上海大学建校100周年陈家泠艺术邀请特展开幕式现场激情地朗诵毛泽东《水调歌头·重上井冈山》，并贺赠《百年上大》书法作品。

I have long aspired to reach for the clouds
And I again visit the city of Shanghai.
Coming from afar to view Shanghai University.
I find new scenes replacing the old.
Everywhere ripply streams babble,
The sound of reading is loud and clear,
And the buildings mount skyward.
Once the library is passed,
No other scenic place calls for a glance.
Wind and thunder are stirring,
Flags and banners are flying
Wherever men live.
A hundred years are fled
With a mere snap of the fingers.
We can clasp the moon in the heaven
And seize turtles deep down in the ocean:
We'll chat about China's revitalization amid song and laughter.
Nothing is hard in this world
If you dare to scale the heights.

陈家泠抄录毛泽东词《水调歌头·重上井冈山》
Chen Jialing copied Mao Zedong's To the Tune of Prelude to
the Melody of Water Reascending Jinggang Mountain

陈家泠赠上海大学建校100周年之《百年上大》
Chen Jialing presented Shanghai University's Centennial Legacy
on the centenary of Shanghai University

久有凌云志，重游上海滩。千里来寻上大，旧貌变新颜。到处潺潺流水，更有书声朗朗，高楼入云端。过了图书馆，美景不胜看。风雷动，旌旗奋，是人寰。一百年过去，弹指一挥间。可上九天揽月，可下五洋捉鳖，谈笑中华兴。世上无难事，只要肯登攀。

上海大学校长、中国工程院院士刘昌胜在"肯登攀"
——纪念上海大学建校100周年陈家泠艺术邀请展特展致辞

Liu Changsheng, President of Shanghai University, Academician of Chinese Academy of Engineering delivered a speech at "Scale the Heights — the invited art exhibition of Chen Jialing" to commemorate the centenary of Shanghai University

On Sep.23, 2022, on the centennial anniversary of Shanghai University, Prof. Chen Jialing, Prof. Xu Genshun and Mr. Chen Liang from Shanghai University jointly held "Scale the Heights" — the invited art exhibition of Chen Jialing to commemorate the centenary of Shanghai University. It includes:

Chen Jialing's "Red Star Shines over Me" — painting and calligraphy exhibition of revolutionary sites, "Ode to the Plum Blossom" — painting and calligraphy exhibition, "Works of Sketching" exhibition, "Scale the Heights" — Exhibition of Xu Genshun's photography works, and Chen Jialing & Chen Liang's Shanghai-style porcelain art exhibition.

上海大学校长、中国工程院院士刘昌胜（中），校党委副书记段勇（左）在陈家泠陪同下参观"红星照我行"——红色革命圣地书画展

Accompanied by Chen Jialing, Liu Changsheng (center), President of Shanghai University, academician of Chinese Academy of Engineering and Duan Yong (left), deputy Party Secretary of Shanghai University visited Red Star Shines over Me—Calligraphy and painting exhibition of revolutionary sites

2022年9月23日，上海大学百年校庆之际，上海大学陈家泠教授、许根顺教授与陈亮联袂举办"肯登攀"——纪念上海大学建校100周年陈家泠艺术邀请特展，其中包括：陈家泠的"红星照我行"——红色革命圣地书画展、"咏梅"书画展、写生作品展，许根顺的"肯登攀"陈家泠艺术足迹摄影作品展，陈家泠和陈亮的海派瓷器艺术展。

上海大学党委副书记欧阳华向许根顺颁予捐赠证书

Ouyang Hua, Deputy Party Secretary of Shanghai University, awarded Xu Genshun a donation certificate

"咏梅"书画展场景
Scene of "Ode to the Plum Blossom" —
Painting and calligraphy exhibition

陈家泠写生作品展场景
Scene of Chen Jialing's "Works of
Sketching" exhibition

陈家泠和陈海派瓷器艺术展场景
Scene of Chen Jialing & Chen Lang's Shanghai-style porcelain art exhibition

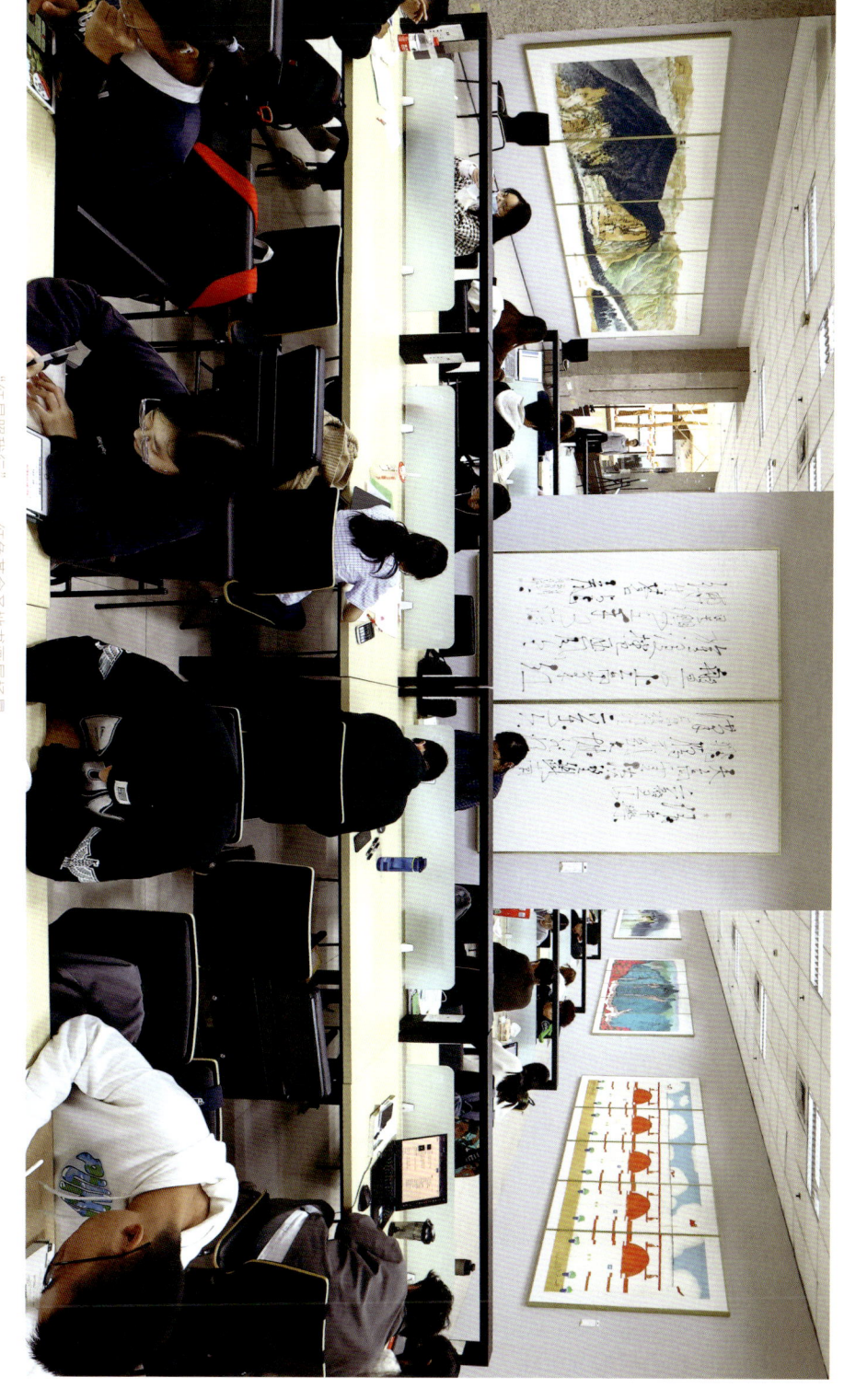

"红星照我行"——红色革命圣地书画展场景
Scene of "Red Star Shines over Me" — Calligraphy and painting exhibition of revolutionary sites

许根顺"青登攀"陈家泠艺术足迹摄影展场景
Scene of "Scale the Heights" — Xu Genshun's photo exhibition

红色圣地

Sacred Places' Revolutionary Heritage

2

Before and after Oct. 2020, Chen Jialing visited twice the Site of the CPC's First National Congress, to sketch and collect materials for artistic creation. He wanted to present his blessing, a "longevity peach" so to speak, to the exhibition marking the centenary of the Communist Party of China. After taking a close look at the birthplace of the Communist Party of China and listening to the guide's introduction attentively, he had a more comprehensive knowledge of the establishment of the Communist Party of China in Shanghai.

The Site of the CPC's First National Congress is the birthplace of the Communist Party of China and the spiritual home of the Chinese communists.

陈家泠在上海中共一大会址纪念馆外景进行资料收集，为创作做充分准备

Chen Jialing visited the Memorial Hall of the Site of the CPC's First National Congress, and collected materials for his artistic creation

2020年10月前后，陈家泠两次来到中国共产党第一次全国代表大会会址（简称一大会址）进行写生，收集创作素材，为中国共产党的百年华诞展览，献上他祝福的"寿桃"。在对中国共产党诞生地认真、仔细参观和聆听讲解员讲解的基础上，他对中国共产党在上海的成立有了一个较全面的认识。

一大会址是中国共产党的诞生地，也是中国共产党人的精神家园。

陈家泠在上海中共一大会址纪念馆实地进行资料收集，为创作做充分准备

Chen Jialing visited the Memorial Hall of the Site of the CPC's First National Congress, and collected materials for his artistic creation

陈家泠上海中共一大会址纪念馆的写生稿
Sketches of the Memorial Hall of the Site of the CPC's First National Congress by Chen Jialing

陈家泠在上海中共一大会址纪念馆写生
Chen Jialing sketched the Site of the CPC's First National Congress

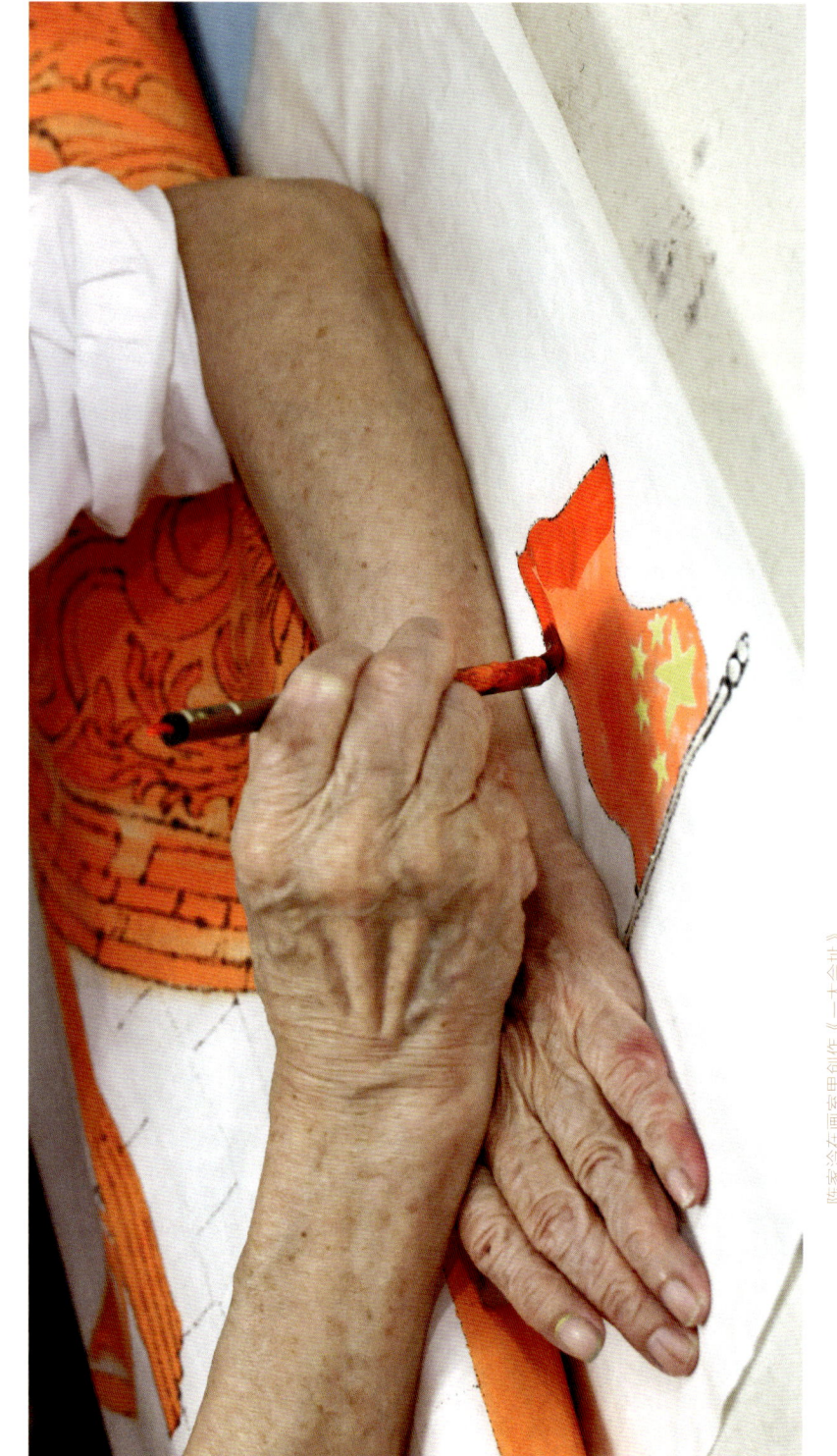

陈家泠在画室里创作《一大会址》
Chen Jialing worked on "The Site of the CPC's First National Congress" in his studio

马家玲 《一大会址》 200cm×100cm×5 2021年
The Site of the CPC's First National Congress by Chen Jialing
200cm×100cm×5 2021

陈家泠在浙江嘉兴南湖红船前留影
Chen Jialing posed in front of the Red Boat in Nanhu Lake, Jiaxing, Zhejiang province

On Dec.11, 2015, Chen Jialing made a special trip to Nanhu Lake, Jiaxing. He boarded the wharf at Nanhu Lake and looked out over the blue rippling lake. The Central Islet was looming in the distance. After stepping onto the islet, he went straight to its top point, and formed a bird's eye view of the islet's surroundings as well as the angle and position of the Red Boat in Nanhu Lake. After sketching and taking photos and collecting relevant materials, he went to the spot where the Red Boat docked, took pictures of and sketched it from various angles. It wasn't until dark that he put away the brush, packed up the camera, and boarded the last ship home, disappearing from the darkness-enveloped lake.

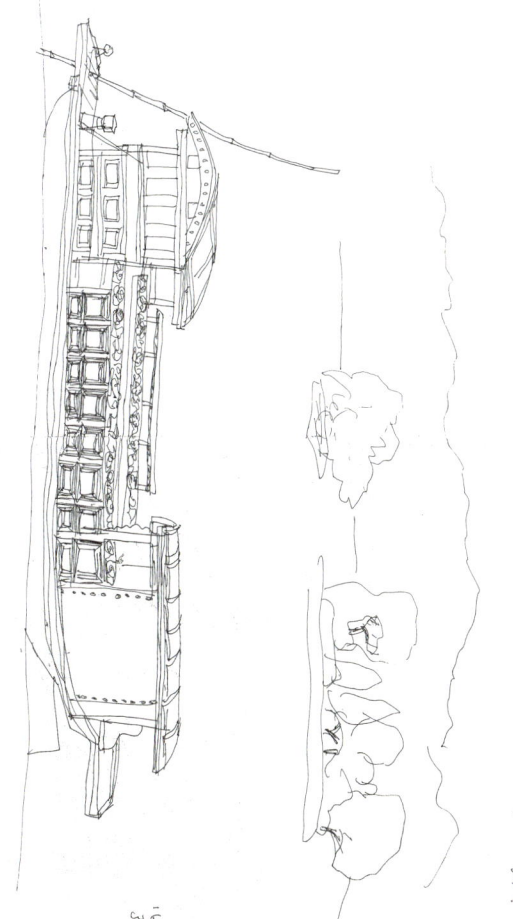

陈家泠浙江嘉兴南湖红船的写生稿
Sketches of the Red Boat in Nanhu Lake, Jiaxing, Zhejiang Province by Chen Jialing

2015年12月11日，陈家泠专程前往嘉兴南湖，登上南湖的码头，眺望着碧波荡漾的湖面，远处的湖心岛便隐隐约约地映入眼帘。上了湖心岛后，陈家泠先直奔小岛山顶，对全岛的四面环境与红船在南湖的角度和位置作了全面的了解并写生、拍照，收集好相关的素材与资料后，便来到红船停靠的位置，进行多角度的写生并拍照，收拾好相机，登上末班游船离开湖心岛，消失在夜色笼罩的湖水中。

陈家泠 《南湖红船》 200cm×100cm×5 2021年
The Red Boat in Nanhu Lake by Chen Jialing 200cm×100cm×5 2021

In preparation for the themed works of the G20 Hangzhou Summit, Chen Jialing went back and forth between Shanghai and Hangzhou, and had to pass through Jiaxing on each round trip. The "Red Boat" on Nanhu Lake in Jiaxing is also an important legacy of CPC's First National Congress.

In July 1921, the delegates of CPC's First National Congress had to be transferred to a pleasure boat on Nanhu Lake, Jiaxing, under the assault of the police in Shanghai French Concession, and resumed the Congress in early August. The delegates discussed and approved on the boat *The First Program of the Communist Party of China* and *The First Resolution of the Communist Party of China*, elected the party's central leading body and proclaimed the founding of the Communist Party of China. Hence Nanhu Lake and the Misty Rain Tower have become one of the witnesses and symbols of the birth of the Communist Party of China, and an integral part of "The Site of CPC's First National Congress", a National Key Cultural Relics Protection Unit.

南湖胜景上

陈家泠为了准备杭州G20的主题作品创作，多次往返于上海、杭州，每次往返都必须经过嘉兴，其中嘉兴南湖红船也是中国共产党第一次全国代表大会的重要遗迹。

1921年7月，因上海法租界巡捕的袭扰，中国共产党第一次全国代表大会与会人员被迫于8月初转移至南湖一条游船上，代表们在游船上讨论通过了《中国共产党的第一个纲领》和《中国共产党的第一个决议》，选举了党的中央领导机构，宣告中国共产党成立。南湖、烟雨楼由此成为中国共产党诞生的见证和象征之一，是全国重点文物保护单位"中共一大会址"的有机组成部分。

陈家泠在西柏坡广场前留影
Chen Jialing posed in front of Xibaipo Square

陈家泠在西柏坡纪念馆的电报墙前留影
Chen Jialing posed in front of the telegraph wall at the Xibaipo Memorial Hall

Chen Jialing is most impressed by the few words in Xibaipo in the northwest of China. It was here that Mao Zedong delivered a report at the Second Plenary Session of the Seventh CPC Central Committee in Mar. 1949. Mao said: We are about to win our victory in the whole country. …There may be some communists, they have never been conquered by an enemy with a gun, and they are worthy of the title of heroes before these enemies. But they can not withstand the attack of sugar-coated cannonballs, they will be defeated by these sugar-coated cannonballs. We must guard against this. Mao also put forward two "musts": "We must keep our comrades modest, prudent, unconceited and unimpetuous. We must see to it that our comrades continue to maintain their style of hard struggle." Chen Jialing often says: The two "Musts" are not only a warning to the whole party, but also the moral we must abide by in our life and work, and the theory we must adhere to in our painting.

陈家泠在西柏坡纪念馆里毛泽东语录"两个务必"前留影
Chen Jialing posed in front of the "Two musts" of Mao Zedong's quotes in the Xibaipo Memorial Hall

在西柏坡有几句话，陈家泠对其印象最深，那就是毛泽东在1949年3月西柏坡召开的七届二中全会上所作的报告，即："我们很快就要在全国胜利了。……可能有这样一些共产党人，他们是不曾被拿枪的敌人征服过的，他们在这些敌人面前不愧英雄的称号；但是经不起人们用糖衣裹着的炮弹的攻击，他们在糖弹面前要打败仗。我们必须预防这种情况。毛泽东还提出了"两个务必"："务必使同志们继续地保持谦虚、谨慎、不骄、不躁的作风，务必使同志们继续地保持艰苦奋斗的作风。"陈家泠经常讲，毛泽东的两个"务必"不仅是告诫全党，也是我们做人、做事的道理，是我们画画的画论。

陈家泠坐小船,在西柏坡的水库中写生
Chen Jialing took a boat to sketch in Xibaipo reservoir

陈家泠在西柏坡对面的山坡上写生
Chen Jialing sketched on the hillside opposite Xibaipo

陈家泠 《西柏坡》 200cm×100cm×5 2021年
Xibaipo by Chen Jialing 200cm×100cm×5 2021

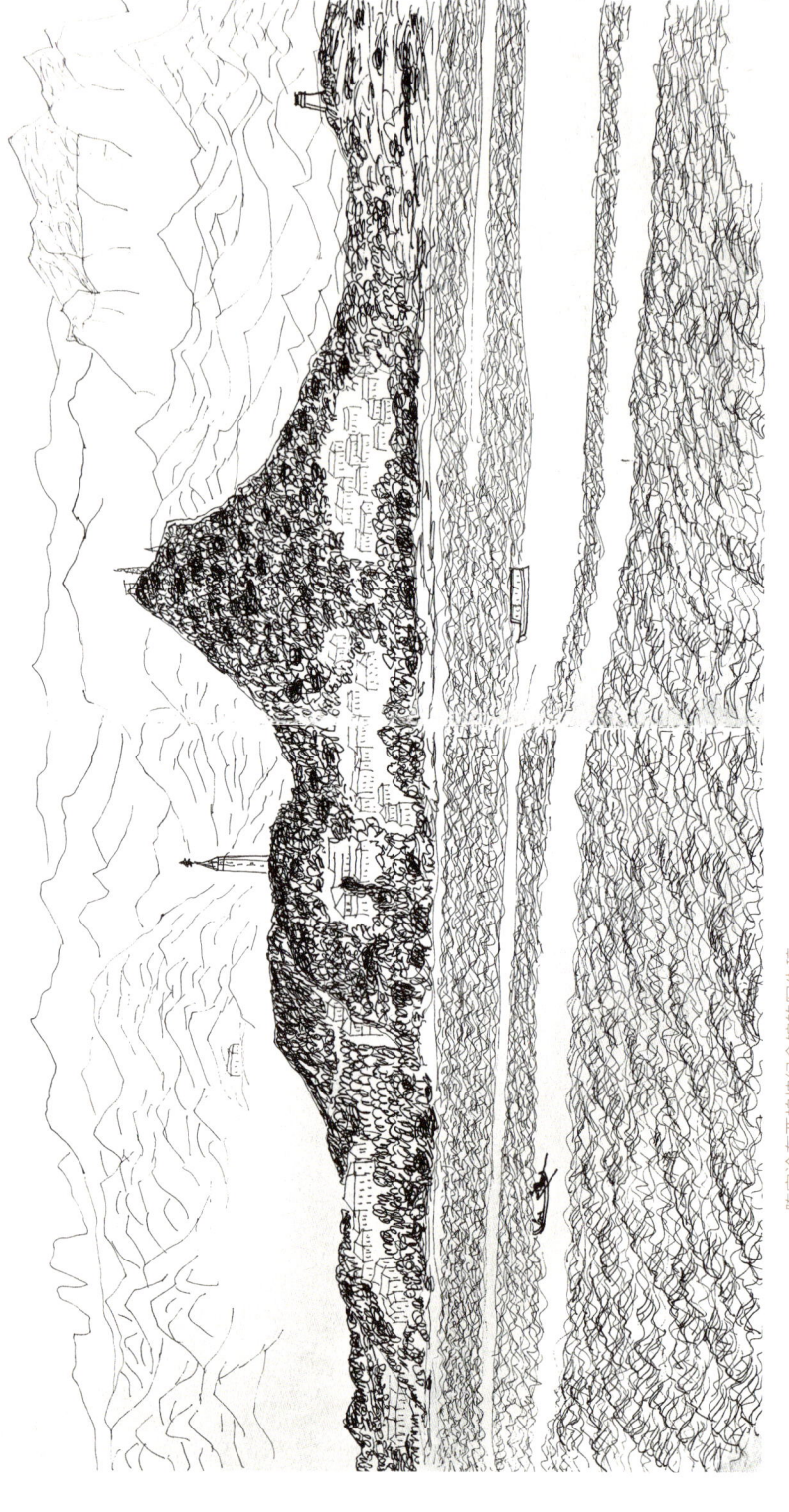

陈家泠在西柏坡纪念馆的写生稿
Sketches of the Xibaipo Memorial Hall by Chen Jialing

陈家泠在上海国际贵都大饭店工作室创作《西柏坡》
Chen Jialing worked on Xibaipo at his studio in Guidu International Hotel, Shanghai

壮丽的井冈山水库
The magnificent reservoir in Jinggang Mountain

On Oct. 27, 2013, Chen Jialing paid his second visit to Jinggang Mountain. His first visit to Jinggang Mountain was actually made in 1960s when he and several of his colleagues in Shanghai Fine Arts School walked all the way from Shanghai to Jinggang Mountain and Shaoshan. In 2013, his first large-scale solo exhibition, "Sublimity", was staged in the National Museum of China. To mark the 120th anniversary of Mao Zedong, at the invitation of Lv Zhangshen, curator of the National Museum of China, he created a painting about Jinggang Mountain for the upcoming exhibition to mark the 120th anniversary of Mao Zedong at the National Museum of China. Shortly after the exhibition, Chen Jialing visited Jinggang Mountain for the second time. This revisit filled him with a myriad of thoughts and emotions. Perhaps it was the passion of fifty years ago that rekindled his boundless feelings. Today, fifty years later, that kind of "When we students are in the flower of our age/Our spirits are higher and more vigorous/" thinking, enriched and strengthened the spiritual connotation of his creation. He climbed every mountaintop in Jinggang Mountain to collect materials for sketching. He even put on an octagonal hat, as if he had heard the assembly call in Luoxiao Mountains.

陈家泠头戴八角帽与雄伟的井冈山合影
Chen Jialing, wearing an octagonal hat, posed in front of the majestic Jinggang Mountain

2013年10月27日，陈家泠第三次上井冈山。其实他第一次上井冈山是在20世纪60年代，当时他和上海大学上海美术学院的几名同事，从上海步行到井冈山和韶山。2013年，他第一次在中国国家博物馆举办"化境"大型个人画展，时值毛泽东诞辰120周年纪念，应时任中国国家博物馆馆长吕章申邀请，创作一幅关于井冈山的作品，参加在中国国家博物馆即将举办的毛泽东诞辰120周年纪念画展。陈家泠在"化境"画展结束后，便马不停蹄地第二次上井冈山。陈家泠重上井冈山，感慨万千，也许是50年前的那种激情，又燃起他无限的情怀，50年后的今天，那种"恰同学少年，风华正茂"的思绪，更加丰富与加强了他的创作精神内涵。他不断地攀登井冈山的每一个山顶，收集写生素材，他还戴起了八角帽，仿佛听到罗霄山脉的集结号。

2013年秋,陈嘉陵相隔50年后再次来到井冈山写生
Chen Jialing returned to Jinggang Mountain to sketch after a gap of 50 years

陈家泠在工作室创作《井冈山主峰》 Chen Jialing was painting *The main peak of Jinggang Mountain* in his studio

陈家冷在井冈山的写生稿
Chen Jialing's sketches of Jinggang Mountain

陈家冷收集拍摄创作资料
Chen Jialing collected materials for filming and creation

陈家泠 《井冈山主峰》 200cm×100cm×5 2021年
The main peak of Jinggang Mountain by Chen Jialing 200cm×100cm×5 2021

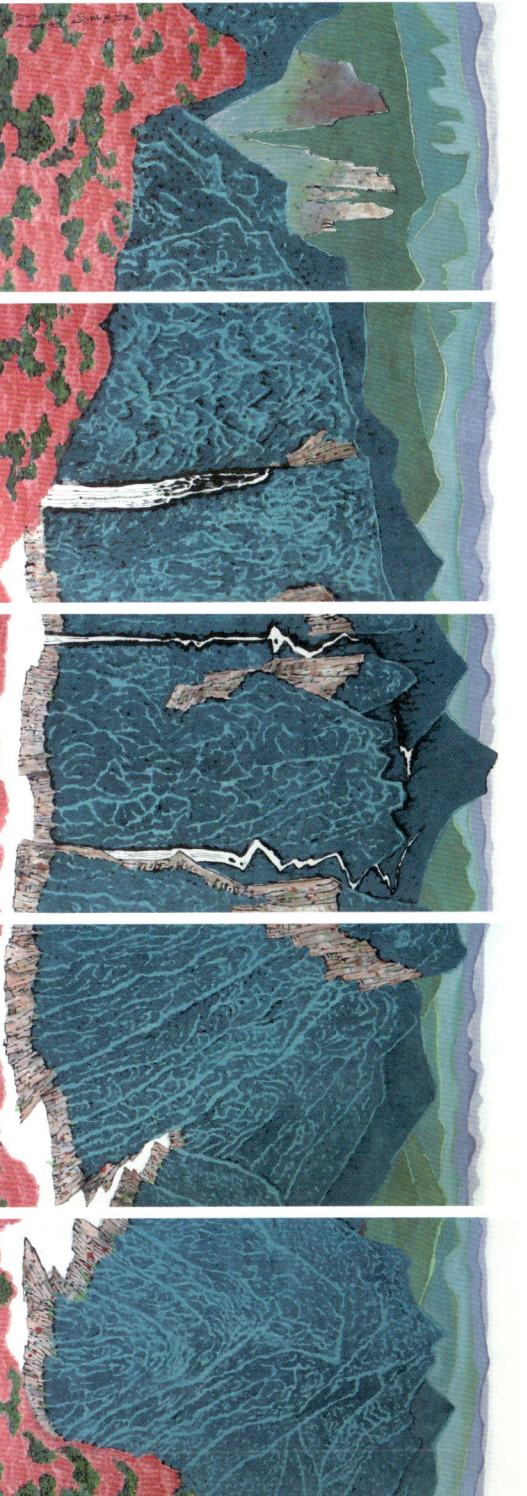

陈家泠在井冈山写生
Chen Jialing sketched in Jinggang Mountain

陈家泠在八角楼收集创作素材
Chen Jialing collected materials for creation at the Octagonal Building

In the autumn of 2013, on his second visit to Jinggang Mountain, Chen Jialing also visited the Octagonal Building in Maoping Village. He painted from the inside to the outside and finally to the back of the Mountain. This photograph was shot from below for a panoramic view. Through thick, towering trees, it put the hero's red clothes and the blue-gray octagonal hat under the white sky, highlighting the dialogue and communication in time and space between man and nature, and between man and history. The one hundred year-old tree tells us about the things and people that happened here in history, the things and people that will always be remembered by New China.

The Octagonal Building is a two-bedroom adobe building behind the Shun Ancestral Hall of the Xie family in Maoping Village. Upstairs there is an octagonal skylight, known locally as the Octagon. From October to November in 1928, Mao Zedong wrote under the oil lamp in the Octagon two glorious works, *Why Can China's Red Regime Exist?* and *The Struggles in Jinggang Mountain*. He summed up the experience of struggles in the revolutionary site of Jinggang Mountain, expounded on the laws governing the development of the Chinese revolution and the basic conditions for the existence and development of the red regime, and put forward the brilliant thought of "The armed independent regime of workers and peasants". The lights of the Octagon illuminated the road to the victory of the Chinese revolution in the dark night.

陈家岭在茅坪村后山上写生
Chen Jialing sketched on the hill behind Maoping Village

2013年秋，陈家岭第二次前往井冈山创作写生时，也去了茅坪村的八角楼，他从室内画到室外，最后又来到后山上继续写生。这幅摄影作品，采用大场面的仰拍，通过茂密的参天大树，把主人公红色的衣服与蓝灰色的八角帽置于白色天光之下，更加突出了人与自然、新中国永远记那些事、那些人。历史上曾经发生在这里的那些事和那些人。

八角楼是在茅坪村谢氏慎公祠后面的一栋土砖土结构的两层楼房，楼上有一个八角形天窗，当地人称之为八角楼。1928年10月至11月，毛泽东在八角楼的油灯下写下了《中国的红色政权为什么能够存在？》《井冈山的斗争》两篇光辉著作，总结了井冈山革命根据地的斗争经验，提出了"工农武装割据"的光辉思想，阐明了中国革命发展的规律，红色政权能够存在和发展的基本条件，八角楼的灯光在茫茫黑夜里照亮了中国革命胜利的道路。

50年前陈家泠（右一）与美校同事从上海步行到韶山（陈家泠提供）
Fifty years ago, Chen Jialing (first right) and his colleagues in Shanghai Fine Arts School walked all the way from Shanghai to Shaoshan (courtesy of Chen Jialing)

In the autumn of 2013, after his second visit to Jinggang Mountain, Chen Jialing went to Mao Zedong's former residence in Shaoshan, Hunan Province for sketching.

2013年10月，陈家泠在韶山毛泽东故居前留影。
Jialing posed in front of Mao Zedong's former residence in Shaoshan, Hunan Province in Oct. 2013

2013年秋，陈家泠第二次前往井冈山创作写生后，去了湖南韶山毛泽东故居写生。

陈家泠在湖南韶山毛泽东故居对面的山坡上写生
Chen Jialing sketched on a hillside opposite Mao Zedong's former home in Shaoshan, Hunan Province

陈家泠在湖南韶山毛泽东故居的写生稿
Sketches by Chen Jialing of Mao Zedong's former home in Shaoshan, Hunan Province

陈家泠《韶山》 200cm×100cm×5 2017年 中国国家博物馆藏
Shaoshan by Chen Jialing 200cm×100cm×5 2017 The National Museum of China

陈家泠在湖南韶山毛泽东故居
Chen Jialing at Mao Zedong's former residence in Shaoshan, Hunan Province

陈家泠在贵州遵义会议纪念馆前留影
Chen Jialing posed in front of the Memorial Hall of
Zunyi Meeting in Guizhou Province

When the famous Marshal Montgomery visited China in 1960, he met Chairman Mao whom he had long admired. He said very humbly that his three famous battles, which he was quite proud of, were inferior to Liaoshen Campaign, Pingjin Campaign and Huaihai Campaign that Chairman Mao commanded. He praised the three campaigns as the best achievements in Chairman Mao's military career. But Chairman Mao corrected him and said, "Crossing the Chishui River Four Times is my crowning feat!"

In order to experience first-hand Mao Zedong's crowning feat, Chen Jialing crossed the Chishui River eight times. He explored the water-side villages, climbed up and down the mountain, trekked the woods and crossed the bridge along the banks of the Chishui River surrounding Bing'an Township. From these "eight crossings", he felt for himself the essence of Mao Zedong's feat, and realized all too clearly the critical importance of the Red Army's arduous endeavor during the Long March, as well as its historical significance in the course of the Chinese Revolution.

陈家泠在贵州"一渡赤水"处留影
Chen Jialing posed at the site of "Crossing the Chishui River for the first time" in Guizhou Province

著名元帅蒙哥马利在 1960 年访华时，见到了他仰慕已久的毛泽东主席。蒙哥马利非常谦逊地讲，自己颇为自得的三场著名战役与毛泽东指挥的辽沈战役、平津战役和淮海战役比起来，还是略逊一筹。为此他盛赞这三大战役是毛泽东军事指挥生涯中的最佳手笔，没想到毛主席纠正他说："四渡赤水才是我的得意之笔。"

为了体悟毛泽东的"得意之笔"，陈家泠围绕丙安古镇的赤水河两岸，水边村寨，山上山下，穿树林过小桥……未来回"八渡赤水"，亲身感受毛泽东"四渡赤水"的精神内涵，亲身体悟红军长征途中"四渡赤水"的艰巨性、艰苦性与关键性及其在中国革命进程中的历史意义。

2016年10月，陈家泠在"四渡赤水"（丙安古镇）的小桥上
Chen Jialing stood on the small bridge of "Crossing the Chishui River Four times" (in Bing'an Township) in Oct. 2016

陈家泠在丙安古镇写生
Chen Jialing sketched in Bing an Township

陈家泠 《丙安古镇之四渡赤水》 200cm×100cm×5 2017年
Crossing the Chishui River Four times in Bing an Township by Chen Jialing 200cm×100cm×5 2017

陈家冷在丙安古镇红军"四渡赤水"的写生稿
Sketches by Chen Jialing of the Red Army's "Crossing the Chishui River Four times" in Bing an Township

红色印象

陈家泠股骨骨折手术后不久，在雨中一级一级地攀登娄山关

Chen Jialing mounted the stone steps of Loushan Pass in the rain, one at a time, after recovering shortly from the femur fracture surgery

In the autumn of 2016, Chen Jialing made a special trip to Loushan Pass in Guizhou Province. It was raining that day, so he had to put on a raincoat and hold an umbrella in one hand. Because he had just recovered from the femur fracture surgery, he would use the umbrella as a crutch from time to time. In the other hand he held a portfolio, and from his neck a camera was hanging. Braving the wind and rain, he mounted the stone steps, one at a time, with great difficulty. Along the way were many monuments, battle sites, and graves of the Red Army martyrs. Everywhere he went he would stop and take a closer look. At this time, rainwater mixed with tears shed for the revolutionary martyrs would run down his cheeks. When he arrived at the battle site of Loushan Pass, facing the Big Gold Mountain, the Small Gold Mountain and the winding mountain road, and looking at the characters "Loushan Pass Battle Site" inscribed on the stone cliffs of Loushan Pass battle site, a tremendous respect for the sacred place of revolution welled up in his heart.

2016年秋，陈家冷专程来到贵州的娄山关。当天下着中雨。他身穿雨衣，一只打伞，一只手拿着画夹，头颈上挂着一个照相机。因为股骨骨折手术痊愈不久，他时而又把伞当作拐杖，另一只手拿着画夹，头颈上挂着一个照相机。顶着风雨，艰难地沿着石阶一步一斜地向上攀登。沿途有不少纪念碑、战斗遗址，还有红军烈士墓。每到一处他都会停下来一一细看。此时他的脸上不知是雨水，还是感怀革命者的壮烈牺牲而留下的泪水。当他来到娄山关大战斗遗址，面对着大金山、小金山与弯曲的盘山公路，以及娄山关大战斗遗址石崖上赫然写着的七个大字"娄山关战斗遗址"时，对红色革命圣地的无限敬意油然而生。

陈家泠在贵州遵义战役实地写生
Chen Jialing sketched at the battlesite of Zunyi in Guizhou Province

Chen Jialing kept pressing the shutter and sketching in the rain, gusts of wind and drops of rain splashing and pattering on his sketchbook. In the end, he finished the most weathered painting on Loushan Pass.

With infinite passion, I recorded with my camera the scene of mountain, wind and rain, distant paths and winding mountain roads. What I recorded most, of course, was my teacher's moves and actions. It is as if we were fighting, fighting and fighting at our own battle sites.

陈家泠冒雨在娄山关写生
Chen Jialing was sketching in Loushan Pass in spite of the rain

陈家泠 《娄山关》 200cm×100cm×5 2017年 中国国家博物馆藏
Loushan Pass by Chen Jialing 200cm×100cm×5 2017 National Museum of China

他不停地按动快门并冒雨写生，风带着雨，雨随着风不停地打落在他的写生本上，最终他完成了娄山关上一幅最具风风雨雨洗礼的创作写生。

我也带着无限的激情记录着这山，这风雨，这情景，还有远处的小路和弯曲的盘山公路，当然更多的是记录老师的镜头，好像此时的我们也在各自的战斗岗位上，战斗，战斗。

陈家泠与许根顺在赤水大瀑布留影
Chen Jialing and Xu Genshun posed at Chishui Falls

On Oct. 16, 2016, Chen Jialing and I went to Chishui Falls in Guizhou Province. Thrilled by the wonders of red sandstone landforms and silver waterfalls, I immediately set up my tripod, placed my camera, and adjusted the aperture and speed. With a pressing on the shutter, a friend took some rare photos of us amidst such a spectacle.

With a height of 76 meters and a width of 80 meters, Shizhangdong Waterfall in Chishui Falls is the largest waterfall in Danxia Landform of China, and the largest waterfall in the Yangtze River valley of the country. The impressive waterfall cascades from the cliff like a million horses galloping. A few miles away, the roaring sound is like thunder; within a few hundred meters, water mist fills the air. Under the sunshine, colorful rainbows appear. Occasionally the gorgeous "Buddha halo" comes into sight, which moves and accompanies the viewer on their way. What a feast for the eyes!

2016年10月16日，我与陈家冷来到贵州赤水大瀑布，面对如此壮观的丹霞与飞瀑奇观兴奋不已，为了能在此留影，我支起三脚架，安好照相机并调好光圈与速度，请朋友只摁快门，果然留下几张十分难得的照片。

赤水大瀑布景区具中的十丈洞大瀑布高76米，宽80米，是我国丹霞地貌上最大的瀑布，也是我国长江流域最大的瀑布。瀑水从悬崖绝壁上倾泻而下，似万马奔腾，气势磅礴，几里之外声如雷鸣，数百米内水雾弥漫，阳光照射之下，呈现五彩缤纷的彩虹，偶尔还能看到奇妙的"佛光环"，随行人移动，一人一环，美不胜收。

陈家泠在贵州千户苗寨写生
Chen Jialing sketched in the One-Thousand-Household Miao Village of Xijiang in Guizhou Province

Located in the Miao and Dong Autonomous Prefecture in the southeast of Guizhou Province, the One-Thousand-Household Miao Village of Xijiang is a famous historical and cultural town in China. It is also an out-door museum, displaying an epic about the development of the Miao ethnic group. The architecture of the One-Thousand-Household Miao Village of Xijiang is a cluster of unique timber-framed stilted buildings constructed in the mid-levels of the mountain. More than 1,000 stilted buildings rise upon one another as the topography changes. They have become the typical village of Miao stilted buildings in the world, and their construction techniques have been included in the first national-level Intangible Cultural Heritage List.

The One-Thousand-Household Miao Village of Xijiang in Guizhou Province presents a picturesque view. In the autumn of 2016, Chen Jialing came here to depict the beauty of China with his paintbrush.

西江千户苗寨地处贵州省黔东南苗族侗族自治州，是中国历史文化名镇。西江千户苗寨，又是一座露天博物馆，展示着一部苗族发展的史诗。西江千户苗寨的建筑是在半山建造独具特色的木结构吊脚楼，千余户吊脚楼随着地形的起伏变化，层峦叠嶂，成为世界典型的苗族吊脚楼村寨，因而西江千户苗寨吊脚楼营造技艺被列入首批国家级非物质文化遗产名录。

西江千户苗寨如诗如画，2016年秋，陈家泠来到贵州千户苗寨，书写大美中国的美丽家园。

陈家泠在贵州荔波写生
Chen Jialing sketched in Libo County, Guizhou Province

Libo County, under the jurisdiction of Buyi and Miao Autonomous Prefecture in the southeast of Guizhou Province, is located at the southernmost tip of the province. Featuring the Karst Landform, it is a beautiful place with towering mountains and rolling hills. In Nov. 2016, Chen Jialing walked on the stone path through the dense jungle in Libo. With streams running at his feet, he kept shooting the scenery of irresistible charm with his camera — up, down, left, right, and collected countless materials for artistic creation.

There are many revolutionary monuments and exhibition halls in Guizhou Province. Chen Jialing visited each of these places like a pilgrim. He watched every piece of the relics carefully and was deeply touched by the Red Army's fighting spirit and lofty faith during that revolutionary period.

荔波隶属于贵州省黔南布依族苗族自治州，地处贵州省最南端，既有高山，也有丘陵，属于喀斯特地貌，是一个山川秀丽的好地方。2016年11月，陈家浴行走在荔波石间的小路，穿梭在茂密的丛林，溪水在脚下哗哗流淌，神仙般美景，只见他的照相机不停地上拍、下拍、左拍、右拍，可见美景对他的吸引力，因此他也收获了无数的创作素材。

贵州有多处红色革命遗址纪念馆、展示馆、陈家浴每到一处，都像朝圣一样，认真仔细地观看，感怀当年红军艰苦卓绝的斗争精神与崇高革命信念。

陈家冷参观红军纪念馆
Chen Jialing visited the Red Army Memorial Museum

陈家泠俯瞰延安全貌
Chen Jialing overlooked the city of Yan'an

In the spring of 2016, in preparation for the grand show to be held at the National Museum of China, Chen Jialing came to Yan'an with infinite respect for the sacred place. He visited the site of the former Central Committee of the Communist Party of China, the Jujube Garden — former Secretariat of the Central Committee of the Communist Party of China, and Pagoda Hill in Yan'an, etc. He visited the places carefully and took notes of them, for all the details would be the source of his creation.

2016年春，为2017年中国国家博物馆大展的创作做准备，陈家泠怀着无限崇敬之情来到延安，他先后参观了中共中央旧址、枣园中共中央书记处旧址、延安宝塔山等。每到一处他都认真仔细地参观并做好记录，因为所有的细节都是他创作的源泉。

陈家谷在延安枣园写生
Chen Jialing sketched in the Jujube Garden, Yan'an

陈家泠在延安宝塔山的宝塔门口留影
Chen Jialing posed at the entrance of the pagoda on Pagoda Hill, Yan'An

In the spring of 2019, Chen Jialing came to Shaanxi. He visited Mausoleum of the Yellow Emperor, Yan'an — the sacred place of Chinese revolution, Hukou of the Yellow River, Liangjiahe and Pagoda Hill in Yan'an, etc. Everywhere he went he sketched and took notes very carefully. For the pagoda on Pagoda Hill in particular, he made detailed records and notes on its modeling structure, fabric style, the introduction of monuments and so forth.

陈家泠 《延安晨韵》 200cm×100cm×5 2017年
中国国家博物馆藏
Charms of Yan'an in the Morning by Chen Jialing
200cm×100cm×5 2017 National Museum of China

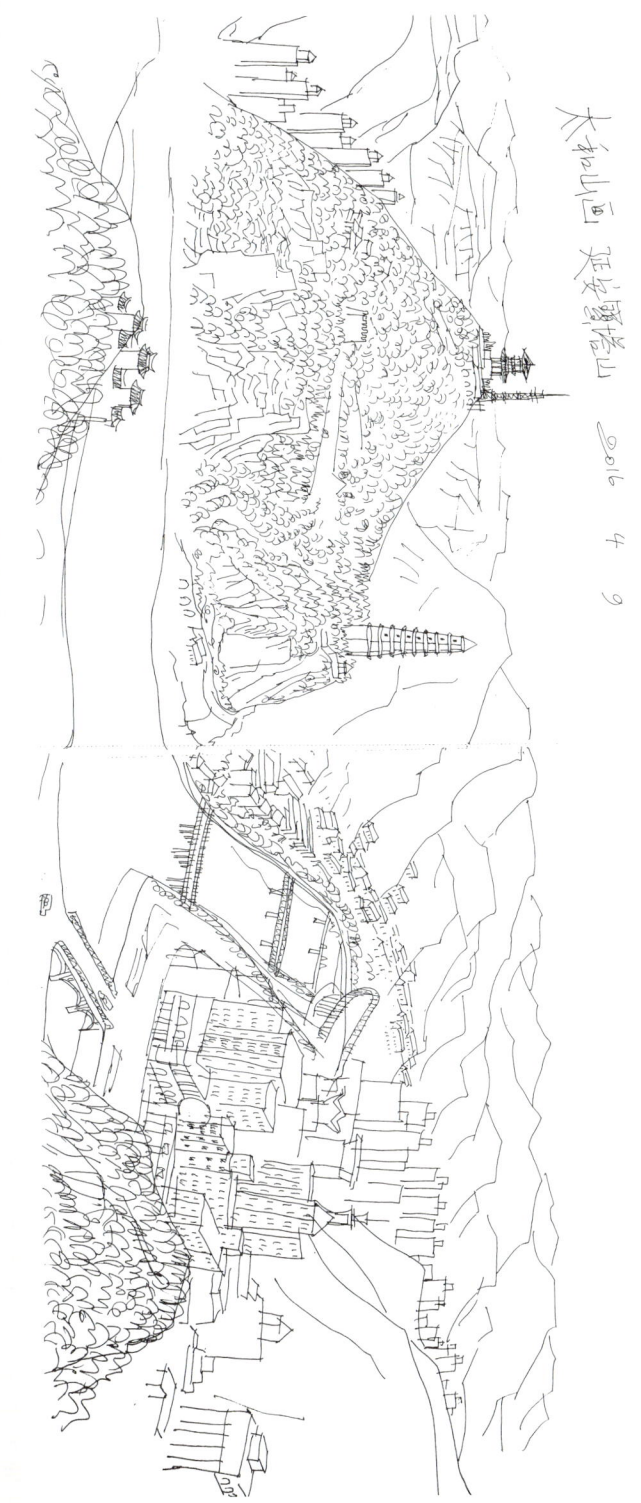

陈家泠在延安的写生稿
Sketches in Yan'an by Chen Jialing

2019年春，陈家泠来到陕西，先后瞻仰了黄帝陵、延安革命圣地、黄河壶口、梁家河和延安宝塔山等。所到之处他都十分认真仔细地写生与记录。特别是对宝塔山上的宝塔，他对塔的造型结构、材质风格、古迹介绍等方面都十分认真地做了详尽的记录与标注。

当年知青们住过的窑洞
The cave dwelling where the educated youth once lived

陈家泠站在高高的山岭上，俯瞰美丽的梁家河
Chen Jialing stood on a high hill overlooking the beautiful Liangjiahe

In Apr. 2016, after having sketched Yan'an for two days, Chen Jialing decided to head for Taihang Mountain as planned. Unexpectedly, the leader of Shaanxi Provincial Tourism Bureau, who accompanied him, suggested that he go to Liangjiahe in Yanchuan for a look. Because of this fortuitous decision, Chen Jialing came to Liangjiahe. The minute he arrived, he was instantly attracted by the momentum of the Loess Plateau in the northwest of China. He quickened his steps, climbed one hill after another, sketching and photographing all the time. It was early spring, and still chilly on the hills, but he seemed to have spotted something and looked eagerly for an angle at the edge of cliff despite a recently-fractured leg and old age. Who knows how happy an artist can be when they stumble upon something that kindles their artistic sensitivity!

Liangjiahe Village, under the jurisdiction of Wen'An Post Town of Yanchuan County, Yan'an City in Shaanxi Province, is located five kilometers southeast of Wen'An Post Town. From the word "Post", we can see that this place has been a vital communications line since ancient times. Walk a few kilometers into the mountains along a newly-built asphalt road south of Wen'An Post Town, and you'll arrive at Liangjiahe Village.

2016年4月，也许是一个偶然的决定，当陈家泠对延安做了两天的写生后，他打算接计划前往太行山。不料同行的陕西省旅游局领导建议可前往延川梁家河看看。陈家泠来到梁家河后，就被黄土高坡的气势深深地吸引了，只见他三步并成两步，登完这山登那山，不停地画着速写，拍摄着山貌。此时正值初春，山上寒意尚存，但他似乎发现了什么，不顾腿部曾骨折且年迈不便，在悬崖边寻找角度，有谁知道，当一个艺术家意外发现了自己找到的艺术感觉是多么高兴啊！

梁家河村，隶属于陕西省延安市延川县文安驿镇，位于文安驿镇东南方向5千米处。从地名上这个"驿"字就可以看出，这里自古就是交通要道。文安驿往南，沿着一条新建的柏油路从山里走几千米，就到了梁家河村。

陈家泠在工作室创作《梁家河,可美啦》
Chen Jialing was working on *Liangjiahe, What a Beautiful Place* in his studio

陈家泠 《梁家河，可美啦》 200cm×100cm×5 2016年
中国国家博物馆藏
Liangjiahe, What a Beautiful Place by Chen Jialing
200cm×100cm×5 2016 National Museum of China

陈家泠在梁家河的写生稿
Sketches in Liangjiahe by Chen Jialing

陈家泠在梁家河收集创作素材
Chen Jialing collected materials for creation in Liangjiahe

陈家泠在太行山写生
Chen Jialing sketched in Taihang Mountain

In Chen Jialing's heart, Taihang Mountain is a solemn monument. Engraved with the achievements of Chinese communists against Japanese aggressors, it is a symbol of the mainstay of the Communist Party of China which led the whole nation in the war of national unity and resistance, and a reflection of the indomitable spirit of a great nation. At the same time, Taihang Mountain presents a breath-taking view of mountains and rivers. Like an impregnable bulwark, the mountain range extends continuously. Chen Jialing made in-depth sketches of Taihang Mountain in Apr. 2016 and autumn of 2020 respectively.

陈家泠在太行山大峡谷写生
Chen Jialing sketched at the Grand Canyon of Taihang Mountain

在陈家泠心中，太行山是一座庄严丰碑，镌刻着中国共产党人的血肉抗战功绩，是中国共产党领导全民族团结抗战的中流砥柱的象征，映射着一个伟大民族顽强不屈的精神。同时，太行山又是一座美丽神奇的山川，如铜墙铁壁，山泉幽长延绵不断。陈家泠分别于2016年4月与2020年秋，对太行山进行了深入的写生创作。

陈家泠在太行山大峡谷玻璃景观平台上写生
Chen Jialing sketched on the all-glass grand viewing platform of the Grand Canyon of Taihang Mountain

In Apr. 2016, Chen Jialing climbed onto the all-glass grand viewing platform of the Grand Canyon of Taihang Mountain, the entire platform is nearly 400 square meters. Standing on the huge transparent glass platform, one has an ecstatic feeling of flying in the air. But for people who suffer a dread of heights, they will be only too terrified to move. Chen Jialing was in high spirits, because this was the perfect vantage point to sketch and overlook the mountains. He walked back and forth on the edge of the glass platform, found a seat, and started drawing right away.

2016年4月，陈家泠来到太行山大峡谷全玻璃观景平台，整个平台面积近400平方米。站在偌大目又通透的玻璃平台上，有一种凌空欲仙的感觉，对于恐高的人而言，则寸步难行，望而生畏。而陈家泠却兴致盎然，因为这里是绝佳的写生角度，一眼望去，群山尽收眼底。他在玻璃平台的最边沿，走了两个来回，找了个座椅，就直接开始画。

陈家泠在太行山写生
Chen Jialing sketched in Taihang Mountain

陈家泠在太行山的写生稿
Sketches by Chen Jialing in Taihang Mountain

陈家泠在太行山写生
Chen Jialing sketched in Taihang Mountain

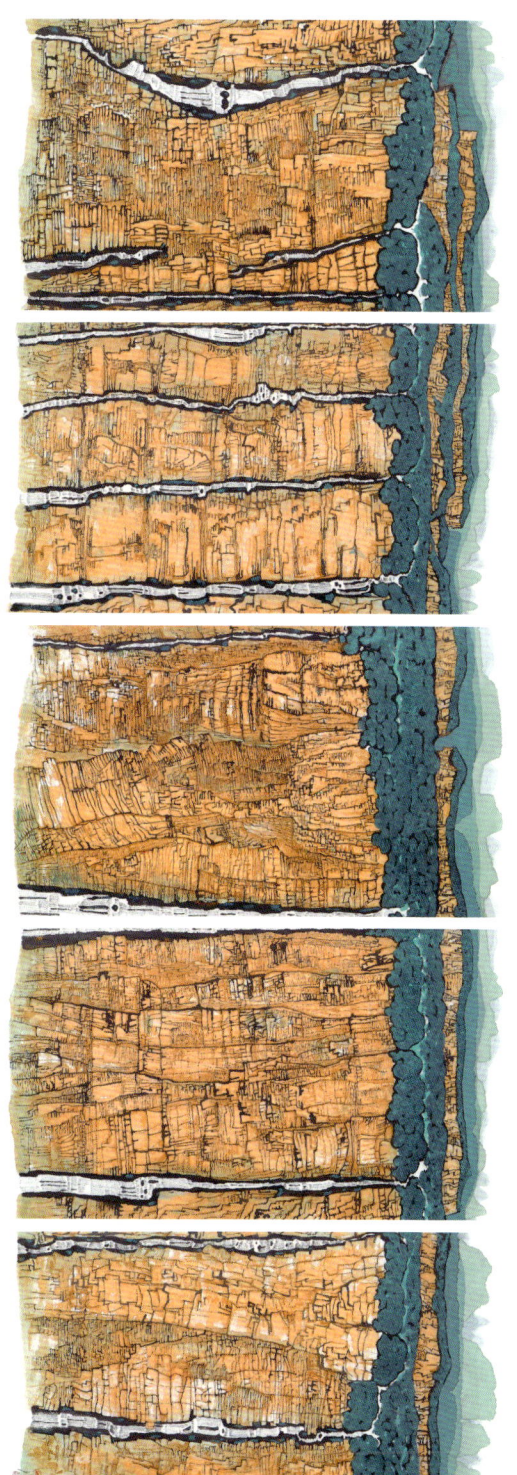

陈家泠 《太行山之铜墙铁壁》
200cm×100cm×5 2017年
中国国家博物馆藏

The Impregnable Bulwark of Taihang Mountain
by Chen Jialing 200cm×100cm×5 2017
National Museum of China

陈家泠在太行山写生
Chen Jialing sketched in Taihang Mountain

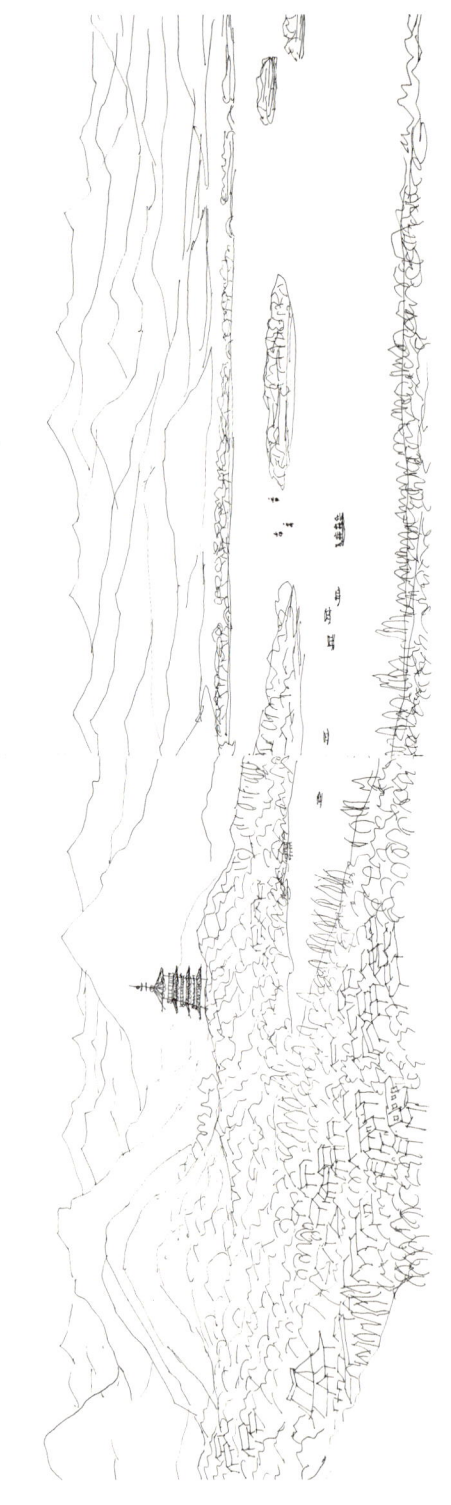

陈家泠西湖景色速写稿之一
One of the sketches of the West Lake landscape by Chen Jialing

2016年5月19日，陈家泠登临杭州城隍阁，为创作G20峰会《西湖景色》收集素材
Chen Jialing climbed onto Chenghuang Pavilion in Hangzhou to collect materials for creating *Landscape of the West Lake* for the G20 summit

Landscape of the West Lake, created by Chen Jialing in the spring of 2016, caused widespread attention. It served as the theme background at the G20 Summit in Hangzhou, China on Sep.4 when Chinese state leaders welcomed the 36 heads of state, heads of government and leaders of international organizations and regions attending the event and took a group photo to mark the occasion, and was preserved in No.1 Hall of Hangzhou Xizi State Guesthouse permanently. His *Landscape of the West Lake II* has been collected by the National Museum of China since 2017.

陈家泠在创作 G20 峰会的主题作品《西湖景色》
Chen Jialing was working on *Landscape of the West Lake*, the theme work of G20 summit

陈家泠 《西湖景色》 200cm×500cm 2016年春
Landscape of the West Lake by Chen Jialing 200cm×500cm Spring, 2016

2016 年春，陈家泠创作的《西湖景色》，在 9 月 4 日中国杭州 G20 峰会上，成为中国国家领导人欢迎出席会议的 36 个国家元首、政府首脑及国际组织和地区领导人并合影留念的主题背景，并永久保存在杭州西子国宾馆一号大厅而被广泛关注。其《西湖景色》二号作品，2017 年被中国国家博物馆收为馆藏。

壮丽祖国
China's Magnificent Landscape

3

陈家泠在太行山采风
Chen Jialing visited Taihang Mountain to collect materials for painting

In the autumn of 2016, Chen Jialing sketched all the way from Guizhou to Shaanxi and from Shaanxi to Shanxi. In the days when he sketched in Taihang Mountain, he was amazed at the precipitous peaks and impregnable massifs, even the trees in the gullies looked exceedingly captivating. Chen Jialing loves to paint trees, especially those that are more than 1,000 years old. From 1,000 year-old, 2,000 year-old, 3,000 year-old, 4,000 year-o d to 5,000 year-old trees, he never fails to sketch and take pictures of them, so he has abundant materials of old trees for painting.

Whether it was a cypress, a gingko or an old mulberry, Chen Jialing was awe-struck by these trees which were rare and nonrenewable treasures in mother nature. Everywhere he went, he would make a point to visit the scenic spots, places of historic and cultural interest, and famous temples and monasteries. Using his paintbrush, he communicated with them, and expressed the unity of man and nature. So during his stay in Taihang Mountain, he would rise early and sleep late every day, and keep painting from morning till night. Sometimes he would venture into the heart of Taihang Mountain, and take photos of the magical trees created by magical nature. There is a picture of him standing next to an oddly-shaped tree. Chen Jialing often says: "My works have all been created from my field trips". Indeed, life is the source of creation. Without a personal involvement in life and close dialogue with nature, artistic works tend to be superficial, lacking vividness and substance.

2016年秋，陈家泠从贵州一路写生到陕西，又从陕西写生到山西。在太行山写生时，不说那陡峭的山峰与铁壁铜墙的山体，就连山涧的树木都千奇百怪。陈家泠喜欢画树，特别是千年以上的古树，从一千年、两千年、三千年、四千年直到五千年的古树，但凡千年古树他必画必拍，所以他的古树素材特别丰富。

无论是柏树、银杏树还是桑树，这些大自然中集聚了精华灵气、不可再生的稀缺瑰宝都吸引着陈家泠。他每到一处，定会对每一个地方的美景及特点、著名历史文化场所、名人名家、名寺院等进行了解、采风。他以无比崇敬的方式，用心灵与其进行沟通，用思想与画笔表达天人合一的化境。因此，在太行山的日子里，每天起早摸黑，从早到晚不停地画。有时他还要深入山腹地。我拍摄的照片中就有一幅他站在一棵造型奇特无比的树边的照片，神奇的大自然造就了神奇的树。陈家泠常说："我的作品都是跑出来的"，生活是创作的源泉，没有深入生活与自然的对话，作品容易概念化，不生动，不接地气。

陈家泠为福建泉州开元寺中1300多年的古桑树题写"桑魂"两字
Chen Jialing worked on the inscription "桑魂"(Mulberry Soul) for the 1,300-year-old mulberry in Kaiyuan Temple, Quanzhou City of Fujian Province

In Mausoleum of the Yellow Emperor, Shaanxi Province, there are Yellow Emperor's "Hand-planted cypress and Life-blessing cypress". In the yard of Songyang Academy, Jinci Temple of Taiyuan, Shanxi Province, there are three "Generals' cypresses" reputed as "living cultural relics".

The thousand-year-old mulberry in Kaiyuan Temple, Quanzhou City of Fujian Province was the oldest in China. Not only was it split into three sections by lightning, but has also produced some white lotus flowers in recent years.

陈家泠正在拍摄山西太原晋祠嵩阳书院内的"将军柏"——"大将军""二将军""三将军"

Chen Jialing took pictures of "Generals' cypresses" in the yard of Songyang Academy, Jinci Temple of Taiyuan, Shanxi Province

在陕西黄帝陵有黄帝"手植柏和保生柏",山西太原晋祠嵩阳书院内有被誉为"活着的文物"的"大将军""二将军""三将军"。

福建泉州开元寺中的千年古桑树,曾被雷劈成了三段,近年还开出过白莲花。

西藏札达县境内十分罕见稀有的一对千年凤凰古树
The rare pair of 1,000-year-old phoenix trees in Zada County, Tibet

At an altitude of 3,700 meters above sea level in Zada, Tibet grows a pair of 1,000-year-old phoenix trees, vigorous and forceful.

在西藏札达县境内海拔3700米处,生长着一对千年凤凰树,苍劲有力。

苏州光福镇"清、奇、古、怪"的两千年古柏树
Four cypress trees of 2,000 years old in Guangfu Town, Suzhou City

Four 2,000-year-old cypress trees in Guangfu Town, Suzhou City are said to have been planted by Deng Yu himself. These four ancient cypresses boast different shapes and postures. Although they have been exposed to bad weather conditions for thousands of years, they are still sturdy and vigorous, like a natural bonsai. A spectacular sight on earth indeed! Legend has it that when Emperor Qianlong of Qing Dynasty visited the southern part of the Yangtze River, he was mesmerized by the four ancient cypresses, and named them "Bizarre", "Odd", "Peculiar" and "Strange" respectively.

苏州光福镇的四株两千年古柏树，相传为邓禹亲手所植。这四株古柏树造型别致，姿态各异，虽经两千年风霜雨雪、日晒雷击的侵袭，却依然遒劲壮观，犹如天然盆景，堪称天下奇绝。据传清代乾隆皇帝下江南巡视来此，被这四株古柏树吸引，叹为观止，分赐它们为"清""奇""古""怪"。

陈家泠 《千年胡杨树》 200cm×100cm×5 2013年 中国国家博物馆藏
1,000-year-old Populus euphratica by Chen Jialing 200cm×100cm×5 2013
National Museum of China

Populus euphratica can withstand the harsh and changeable climate of drought in the desert. Extremely tolerant of saline soil, it is one of the rare tree species in nature. Populus euphratica is also one of the oldest poplar trees in the world. It thrives in Taklamakan Desert with high levels of salt in the ground water.

陈家泠在新疆麦盖提县塔克拉玛干沙漠中的千年"胡杨恐龙"前写生
Chen Jialing sketched in front of a 1,000-year-old tree called "Populus euphratica dinosaur" at Taklamakan Desert at the Karamakan site in Markit, Xinjiang

胡杨能承受沙漠中干旱、多变的恶劣气候，对盐碱地的忍耐力极强，是自然界稀有的树种之一。胡杨是世界上最为古老的一种杨树，在地下水含盐量很高的塔克拉玛干沙漠，它照样枝繁叶茂。

陈家泠钻进潮湿阴暗又粗大的神木中,寻找最佳拍摄角度
Chen Jialing delved into the damp, dark and thick sacred tree to find the best angle for shooting

On the main peak of Ali Mountain in Taiwan stands a huge tree. Its trunk leans slightly, its main stem is broken, but its branches are verdantly green. Being about 52 meters tall and about 23 meters thick, it takes more than a dozen people to wrap their arms around it. Towering, vigorous and lush, it is revered as the "Sacred Tree of Ali Mountain".

台湾阿里山的神木
The sacred tree of Ali Mountain in Taiwan

在台湾阿里山主峰耸立着一棵大树，树身略倾侧，主干已折断，但树梢的分枝却苍翠碧绿，树高52米左右，树围约23米，需十几人才能合抱，巍巍挺立，苍劲葱郁，被人们尊为"阿里山神木"。

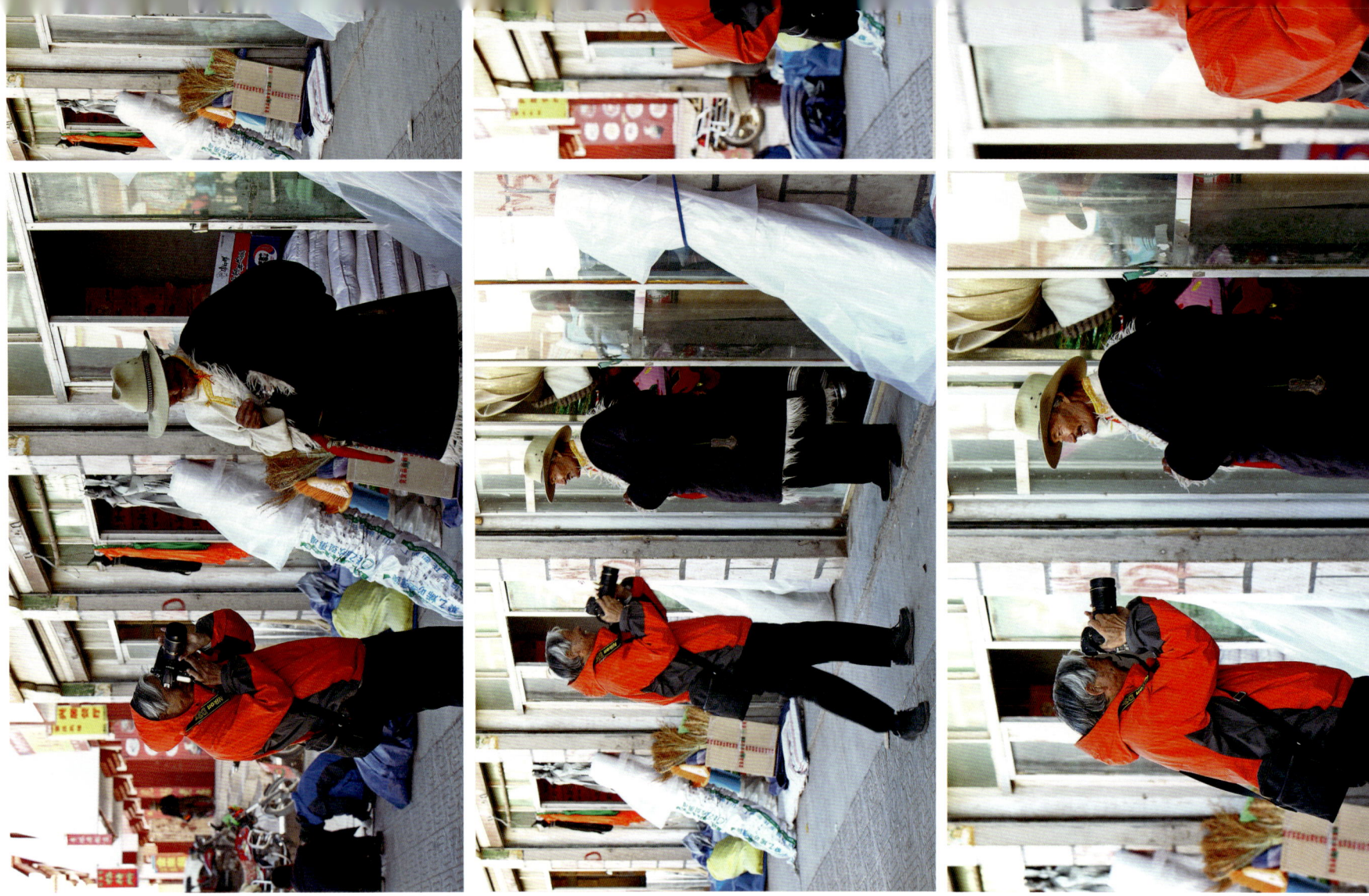

2012年7月,陈家泠在西藏拍摄,跟、抓拍人物的整个摄影过程
The whole process of photographing a local herdsman in Tibet by Chen Jialing in July 2012

Compared with other types of feature photography, portrait photography is the most difficult and elusive. The characters have a lot of expressions and movements. The use of lighting attaches importance to multiple visual representations while the color composition lays emphasis on multiple themes. For facial expressions alone, there are pleasure, anger, sorrow, joy, etc. For composure, there are calmness, ease, arrogance, generousness, happiness, angriness, etc. And for looks, there are stare, glare, glance, gaze, glimpse, etc. Therefore, to get the hang of portrait photography one must grasp four elements. First, one must fully grasp the flexible use of the technique, performance and characteristics of photography equipment. Second, one must have a sharp eye and good physical quality to choose, wait, snap and capture a shot. Third, one must have keen senses to explore beauty and good judgments of picture composition. Fourthly, one must have the foresight to turn every fleeting moment into exquisite works.

人物摄影相对于其他专题摄影而言，难度最大，变化最多，人物表情丰富且动作多样，用光讲究画面多，色彩构图主题多。仅表情就有：喜、怒、哀、乐等，神态就有：镇定、自如、傲气、大气、高兴、生气等，其眼睛就有：朝向、专注、表达、精神等。所以对于人物摄影就必须掌握四要素：一是要对摄影器材的技术、性能、特点充分把握，灵活运用；二是要有挑、等、抢、抓的敏锐眼光和良好的身体素质；三是要有一双能发掘美的好眼睛与把握画面构图的判断力；四是要有预判性，能把精纵即逝的每一个瞬间变为精美的作品。

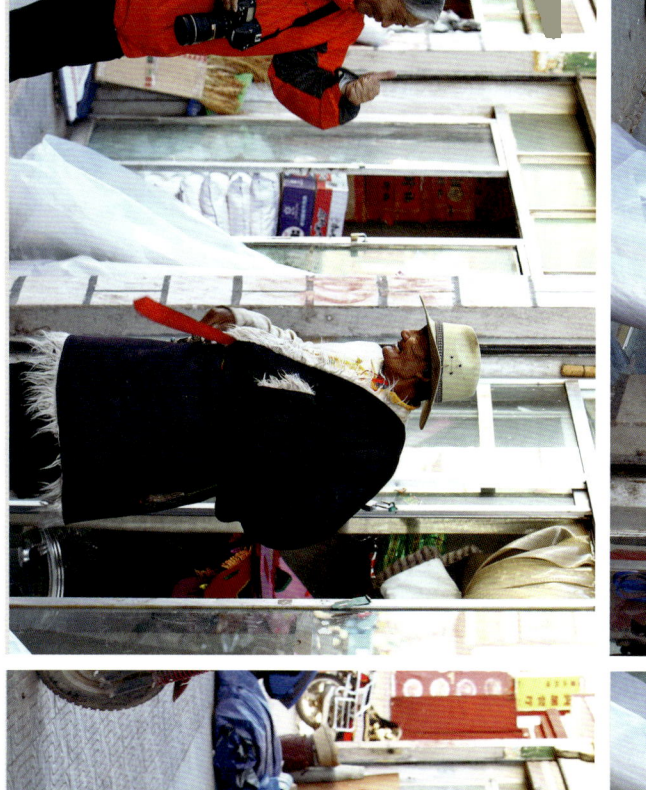

陈家泠拍摄后与藏族老人亲切交谈
Chen Jialing chatted genially with Tibetan old man after photographing

陈豪冷在西藏区牧民的帐篷里拍照
Chen Jialing took pictures in a Tibetan herdsman's tent

In July 2012, on his way to the Ali region in Tibet Autonomous Region, Chen Jialing passed two herdsmen's tents. He immediately stopped to pay a visit to the local herdsmen on the grassland. After exchanging greetings and making known his intention, Chen Jialing was warmly invited into the tent by the herdsmen. The living facilities of the herdsmen in the tent were very poor, beams of light from the top of the tent mixed with the smoke from the cooked yak butter tea, forms a distinctive pastoral atmosphere and presents the life sentiments of Tibetan herdsmen. This kind of herdsmen and living scene in Tibet was exactly what Chen Jialing was looking for. So he sketched and took pictures of the old herdsman and the little girl, as well as all the living facilities inside and outside the tent carefully.

2012年7月,陈家泠在西藏自治区前往阿里地区的途中,路过两顶牧民的帐篷,当即停车拜访了当地草原上的牧民。经过交流,陈家泠被牧民热情地邀请到帐篷中做客。帐篷中牧民的生活设施十分简陋,缕缕光束从篷顶外透进来,融进烧煮酥油茶的烟气中,形成牧区特有的氛围,别有一番藏区的牧民生活情调。这种藏区的牧民与生活场景,正是陈家泠寻找的。于是他对着老牧民与牧民小女孩以及帐篷内外的所有生活设施都认认真真,仔仔细细地写生和拍照。

陈家泠艰难地在西藏古格王朝遗址的古道上不断攀登
Chen Jialing climbed with difficulty onto the ancient road of the Guge Dynasty ruins in Tibet

In July 2012, Chen Jialing came to Tibet, where he confronted the Guge Dynasty ruins — a mountain-like castle located at nearly 4,000 meters above sea level and full of caves and tunnels. This castle was designed to keep out foreign invaders. Houses and caves, like mazes, are easy to defend but hard to attack. In order to record these, 75-year-old Chen Jialing overcame hypoxia on the plateau and climbed from the bottom to the top for sketching.

2012年7月，陈家泠在西藏，身处海拔将近4000米，到处是洞窟与暗道，像山一样的城堡——古格王朝遗址。这座城堡是为了抵御外来入侵者而精心设计的。房屋与洞窟，像迷宫一样，都是易守难攻的。为了记录这些，75岁高龄的陈家泠克服高原缺氧，由下而上地攀登，进行创作写生。

陈家泠在西藏穿越古格王朝遗址的时光岩洞
Chen Jialing walked through the time caves of the Guge Dynasty ruins in Tibet

陈家泠在古格王朝遗址上收集创作素材
Chen Jialing collected materials for creation at the Guge Dynasty ruins in Tibet

陈家泠站在西藏古格王朝遗址上远眺
Chen Jialing stood on the Guge Dynasty ruins in Tibet overlooking the scene

陈家泠在古格王朝遗址上收集创作素材
Chen Jialing collected materials for creation at the Guge Dynasty ruins in Tibet

太阳余晖下的古格王朝遗址周边的山脉与古老的寺院
The sun glowed over the mountains and ancient monasteries surrounding the Guge Dynasty ruins

This is a very precious photo recording the sketching scene of Chen Jialing, and an excellent photographic work as well. In order to get this shot, I lay on my stomach and shot from a low angle. When the 75-year-old Chen Jialing jumped into the air, I quickly pressed the shutter. It was nothing short of an accomplishment to leap into the sky with such a dashing and domineering action on the plateau 4,000 meters above sea level.

这是一幅记录陈家泠写生场景十分珍贵的照片,也是一张极佳的摄影作品。为了拍摄好这一张照片,我整个人趴在地上,通过低角度仰拍。当75岁高龄的陈家泠一跃而起的时候,我敏捷地按下快门。在4000多米的高原之上冲天一跳,动作如此潇洒、霸气,实在难得。

拍摄者:许根顺
时间:2012年7月15日上午
人物与地点:陈家泠 背景西藏扎达古格王朝遗址
相机、型号:Canon EOS 5D Mark IV
F:7.1 ISO:320 速度:1/500 焦距:35mm

Photographer: Xu Genshun
Time: On the morning of July 15, 2012
Character & Place: Chen Jialing, Guge Dynasty ruins in Zada, Tibet
Camera model: Canon EOS 5D Mark IV
F: 7.1 ISO: 320 Speed: 1/500 Focus: 35mm

陈家泠与许根顺在西藏羌塘国家级自然保护区留影,背景是雪山和冰川
Chen Jialing and Xu Genshun posed for a photo at Qiangtang Nature Reserve in Tibet, with the snow mountain and glacier

Qiangtang Nature Reserve is located in Nacu and Ali regions of Tibetan Autonomous Region, its coordinates are 79°42'-92°05' East longitude and 32°10'-36°32' North latitude. The Nature Reserve is surrounded on three sides by Kunlun Mountain Ranges in the north, Karakoram Mountain Ranges in the west and Gangdise-Nyainqentanglha Mountain Ranges in the south. The average altitude is about 5,000 meters above sea level.

This is my second trip to Tibet, the first time was in July 1985 when I had a three-month internship at *Tibet Daily* after graduating from Journalism Department of Jiangxi University. This time I came to shoot *Chen Jialing*, a wide-screen documentary in color for Shanghai Film Studios.

陈家泠在西藏羌塘国家级自然保护区留影
Chen Jialing posed for a photo at Qiangtang Nature Reserve in Tibet

西藏羌塘国家级自然保护区位于西藏自治区的那曲地区和阿里地区，地理坐标为东经79°42'—92°05'，北纬32°10'—36°32'，其北、西、南三面分别为昆仑山脉、喀喇昆仑山脉和冈底斯—念青唐古拉山脉所环绕，平均海拔5000米左右。

这是我第二次进藏，第一次是1985年7月江西大学新闻系毕业时在《西藏日报》实习3个月，这一次是为上海电影制片厂拍摄《陈家泠》彩色宽银幕纪录片而来的。

陈家泠在玛旁雍错留影
Chen Jialing posed for a photo at Lake Manasarovar

Located in Burang County, Tibet, Lake Manasarovar is surrounded by beautiful natural scenery, and its average altitude is 4,500 meters above sea level. It is the most transparent freshwater lake in China and the birthplace of four major rivers in Asia.

Mount Kailash is one of the four sacred mountains of Tibetan Buddhism, Lake Manasarovar is located 20 Kms southeast of Mount Kailash. Monk Xuanzang of the Tang Dynasty claimed in *Collecting Scriptures in Tenjiku* that Lake Manasarovar was the site of Jasper Lake, a legendary dwelling place where the Queen Mother of the West in Chinese mythologies lived.

In the summer of 2012, Chen Jialing came to Lake Manasarovar. Looking at the rippling blue water, he felt a cleansing of souls and a baptism of life.

陈家泠在玛旁雍错留影
Chen Jialing posed for a photo at Lake Manasarovar

玛旁雍错在西藏普兰县境内,其周围风光优美,平均海拔4500米,是中国湖水透明度最大的淡水湖,也是亚洲四大河流的发源地。

冈仁波齐峰是藏传佛教四大神山之一。玛旁雍错位于冈仁波齐峰东南20千米处。唐代玄奘在《大唐西域记》中称玛旁雍错是西天王母瑶池之所在。

2012年夏,陈家泠来到玛旁雍错,望着碧波荡漾的湖水,感受到一种心灵的净化与人生的洗礼。

神秘而又神圣的冈仁波齐峰
Mysterious and sacred Mount Kailash

陈家泠在玛旁雍措拍照
Chen Jialing took photos at Lake Manasarovar

陈家泠在西藏阿里无人区
Chen Jialing at the depopulated zone of Ali in Tibet

For days, our car had been driving in the 5,000-meter-high depopulated zone of Ali in Tibet. Apart from the peaks, snow-capped mountains, glaciers, sacred lakes and vast prairies, in the morning you will also see groups of wild horses, Tibetan antelopes and ducks frolicking in the lake, which gives you a feeling of excitement as if you were taking an adventure in a different world. While sketching on his way to the depopulated zone in Tibet, Chen Jialing encountered both sunny and cloudy days. One moment there were thunder and lightning, the next colorful rainbows appeared. More amazingly, several weather conditions could appear in the same piece of sky at the same slot of time. It is no exaggeration that there are four seasons within the mountain and competing weathers within ten miles.

汽车多天一直行驶在海拔5000米茫茫的西藏阿里无人区,除了群群峰、雪山、冰川、神湖和一望无边的大草原外,清晨你还会看到一群群野马、藏羚羊和湖中一群群嬉戏的野鸭,有一种置身世外探险的刺激感。陈家浴在西藏无人区途中写生,还遇见了阴晴两重天——时而电闪雷鸣,时而彩虹高挂,更神奇的是这几种天气状况会同时出现在一片天空中,真是一山有四季,十里不同天。

西藏阿里无人区
The depopulated zone of Ali in Tibet

Chen Jialing was intoxicated in the mystery before him. Marveling at the breath-taking view, he kept exclaiming and pressing the shutter. Sometimes, he would simply ask the driver to stop and take out his sketchbook. He sketched passionately facing the rare landscape of snow peaks on the plateau, and regarded these sketches as the biggest gain of his day.

陈家泠在西藏阿里无人区
Chen Jialing was at the depopulated zone of Ali in Tibet

陈家泠始终陶醉在眼前的秘境之中，不断地发出无限的感慨又不停地按动着快门。有时，干脆要求停车，拿出写生本，面对十分难得的高原雪峰景观进行写生，他把这种充满激情的写生，看成他一天中最大的收获。

陈家珍在吾金扎普写生
Chen Jialing sketched in Wujin Zhapu

陈家泠探洞
Chen Jialing explored the cave

陈家泠在吾金扎普天然溶洞中探险（左右页组图）
Chen Jialing explored the natural cave in Wujin Zhapu

陈家泠钻洞
Chen Jialing crawled through the natural cave

Chen Jialing has crawled through the natural cave in Wujin Zhapu (meaning "sacred cave" in Tibetan) where Padmasambhava practiced. It is deep and long, and some holes are so narrow that only one person at a time can get himself out sideways by pushing his feet, which is too hard for fat people. Dark and slippery inside, the cave's natural stalactites, in various shapes, have been given religious significance by believers. Chen Jialing was pulled out slowly by his son through a small and narrow hole, the whole process felt like rebirth.

陈家泠从一个小小的洞口中艰难地露出头部
Chen Jialing's head emerged from a small hole with difficulty

陈家泠的儿子陈亮配合父亲小心翼翼地从洞中爬出来
Chen Liang, Chen Jialing's son, carefully pulled his father out of the cave

陈家泠钻过的吾金扎普（藏语，意为神仙洞），是莲花生大士修行过的天然溶洞，既深又长，甚至有些地方只能一人侧身用脚使劲蹬出来。体型稍胖的人还钻不出来。洞内阴暗湿滑，溶洞内天然形成的形状各异的钟乳石被信徒们赋予宗教意义。陈家泠便是从一个既小又有些形状的洞口由他儿子慢慢地拉了出来，整个过程有一种重生的感觉。

陈家泠在马攸木拉山垭口留影
Chen Jialing posed for a photo at the pass of Mayoumula Pass

In July 2012, Chen Jialing started his tour around Tibet after finishing his film-making mission there. Coming to Tibet was a challenge by itself, so why not take a nice long walk through Tibet after he had finally overcome the high altitude hypoxia? By filming and sketching Tibet in its entirety, he could accumulate more materials for later creation. Hence his unforgettable immersion tour of Tibet began.

Mayoumula Pass, located in Burang County, Tibetan Autonomous Region, is the border between Shigatse District and Ali. Once you pass it, you enter Burang County of Ali. The mountain pass commands a good view and the vast alpine meadows are deserted. Mayoumula Pass is 5,211 meters above sea level. In this no-man's land, wild animals such as Tibetan antelopes can often be seen running on the high mountains.

2012年7月，陈家泠在结束了西藏的电影摄制任务后，便开启了自己的西藏之旅。因为到西藏是一件十分不容易的事，好不容易刚刚渡过了高原缺氧关，何不在西藏好好地走着看，认真仔细地对西藏做一个全面的拍摄和写生记录，为以后的创作积累更多的素材。于是就有了他终身难忘的沉浸式西藏之旅。

马攸木拉山口，位于西藏自治区普兰县境内，是日喀则和阿里的分界点。过了这个山口，就进入阿里的普兰县。山口视野较好，广阔的高山草甸荒无人烟，马攸木拉垭口海拔5211米，在这片无人区经常能看到在高山上奔跑的藏羚羊等野生动物。

陈家岭朝着希夏邦马冰川走去
Chen Jialing walked towards the Xixiabangma Glacier

Mount Xixiabangma is 8,027 meters above sea level, the 14th highest among the fourteen 8,000-kilometer peaks in the world. It is also an 8,000-kilometer peak completely within Chinese territory. About 120 kilometers southeast of Mount Qomolangma, in Nyalam County, Tibet, it is one of the centers of modern glaciation in the Himalayas, a place where giant avalanches occasionally happen.

希夏邦马峰海拔8027米，在世界上14座8000米级高峰中排名第14位，也是一座完全在中国境内的8000米级山峰。东南方距珠穆朗玛峰约120千米，在西藏聂拉木县境内，这里是喜马拉雅山脉现代冰川作用的中心之一，在这里时而会发生雪崩。

珠穆朗玛峰远眺
A distant view of Mount Qomolangma

陈家泠在新疆喀什天门大峡谷
Chen Jialing was in Tianmen Grand Canyon in Kashgar, Xinjiang

Tianmen Grand Canyon in Kashgar, Xinjiang is about 30 kilometers long. High Cliffs on both sides, the mountain was formed as if torn by force. It is an exhibition hall and geological museum of the changes in geological and crustal movements in China and even the world.

新疆喀什天门大峡谷全长约 30 千米,两侧断壁高耸,山体犹如强行撕裂而成,是中国乃至全球地质地壳运动变化的展览馆和地质博物馆。

2014年秋，陈家泠在新疆塔格拉玛干沙漠中收集胡杨树创作素材
In the autumn of 2014, Chen Jialing collected materials of populus euphratica for creation in Tagramakan Desert of Xinjiang

Makit County is part of the Kashgar region of Xinjiang Uygur Autonomous Region, to its east are Taklamakan Desert and Hotan Prefecture. Located on the edge of the desert, Makit County has an obvious continental climate characterized by abundant heat, plentiful sunshine, sharp temperature difference between day and night, and little precipitation.

麦盖提县隶属新疆维吾尔自治区喀什地区，东临塔克拉玛干大沙漠与和田地区。麦盖提县地处沙漠边缘，大陆性气候十分明显，热量丰富，日照充足，昼夜温差大，降水量极少。

2014年秋，陈家泠在新疆麦盖提的刀郎千岛湖收集创作素材
In the autumn of 2014, Chen Jialing collected materials for creation in the Thousand-Island Lake of Daolang in Makit County, Xinjiang

The Thousand-Island Lake of Daolang in Makit County boasts a vast expanse of water like a mirror set in the boundless desert, presenting a fantastic scene. On the bank willows droop, and the lake is as clear as emerald. The blue sky and white clouds are reflected in the water, blending in one color, too beautiful to be absorbed all at once. Early in the morning, the misty water is soft and blue, and the mist is flowing on the lake, adding a bit of mystery. Placing himself in the midst of reed marshes, Chen Jialing, dressed in a bright red waistcoat, glowed against the backlight and the reed blossom.

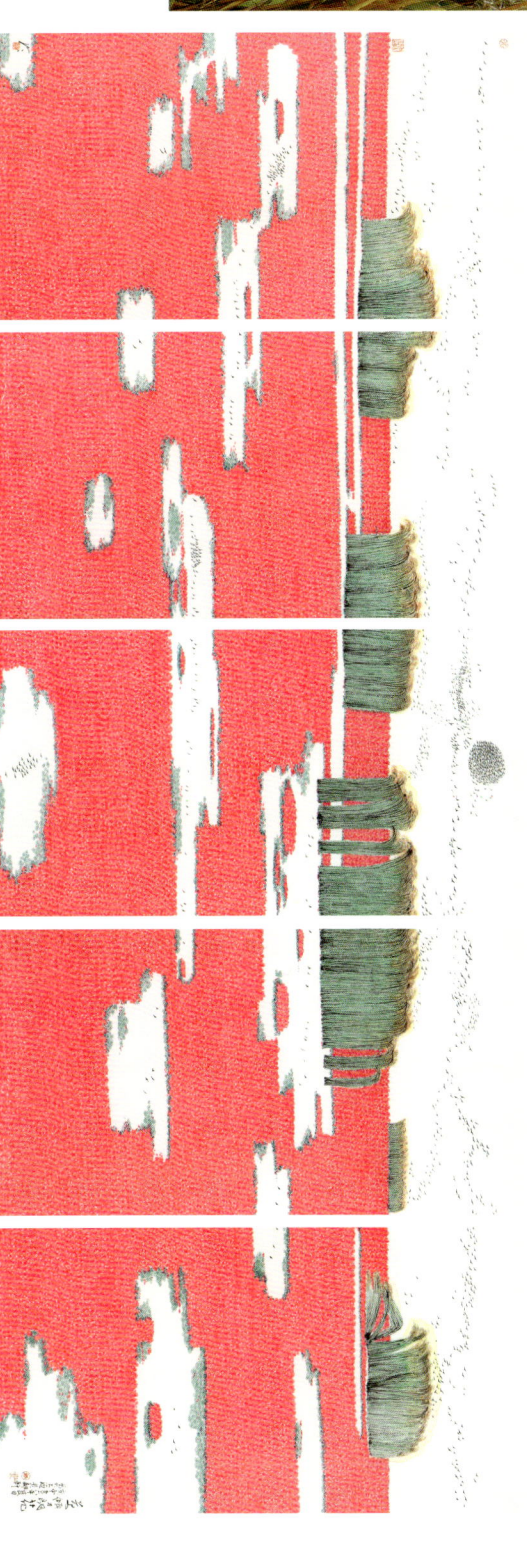

陈家泠 《万顷刀郎湖》 200cm×100cm×5 2013年 中国国家博物馆馆藏
The Vast Expanse of Daolang Lake by Chen Jialing 200cm×100cm×5 2013 National Museum of China

麦盖提县的刀郎千岛湖水域辽阔，宛如明镜镶嵌在茫茫大漠，此番绝景，令人称奇。岸边杨柳低垂，湖水清澈见底，碧如翡翠。蓝天白云倒映水中，水天一色，美不胜收。每逢清晨，轻雾弥漫的湖水温柔、碧蓝，薄雾在湖面飘动，更增添了些许神秘。芦苇荡中的陈家泠，身着艳红色的马甲，在逆光与芦花的映衬下气色绽放。

陈家泠在黄山写生
Chen Jialing sketched in Mount Huangshan

Located within Huangshan City in the southern part of Anhui Province, Mount Huangshan has 72 peaks. One of its main peaks, the Lotus Peak, has an elevation of 1,864.8 meters. Together with Guangming Peak and Tiandu Peak, they are known as the three main peaks of Mount Huangshan. It is said that "You have no wish to visit any other mountain after returning from a trip to the Five Mountains, and you have no wish to visit the Five Mountains after returning from a trip to Mount Huangshan." Mount Huangshan deserves such a reputation.

黄山在安徽省南部黄山市境内,有七十二峰,主峰莲花峰海拔1864.8米,与光明顶、天都峰并称三大黄山主峰,素有"五岳归来不看山,黄山归来不看岳"的美称。

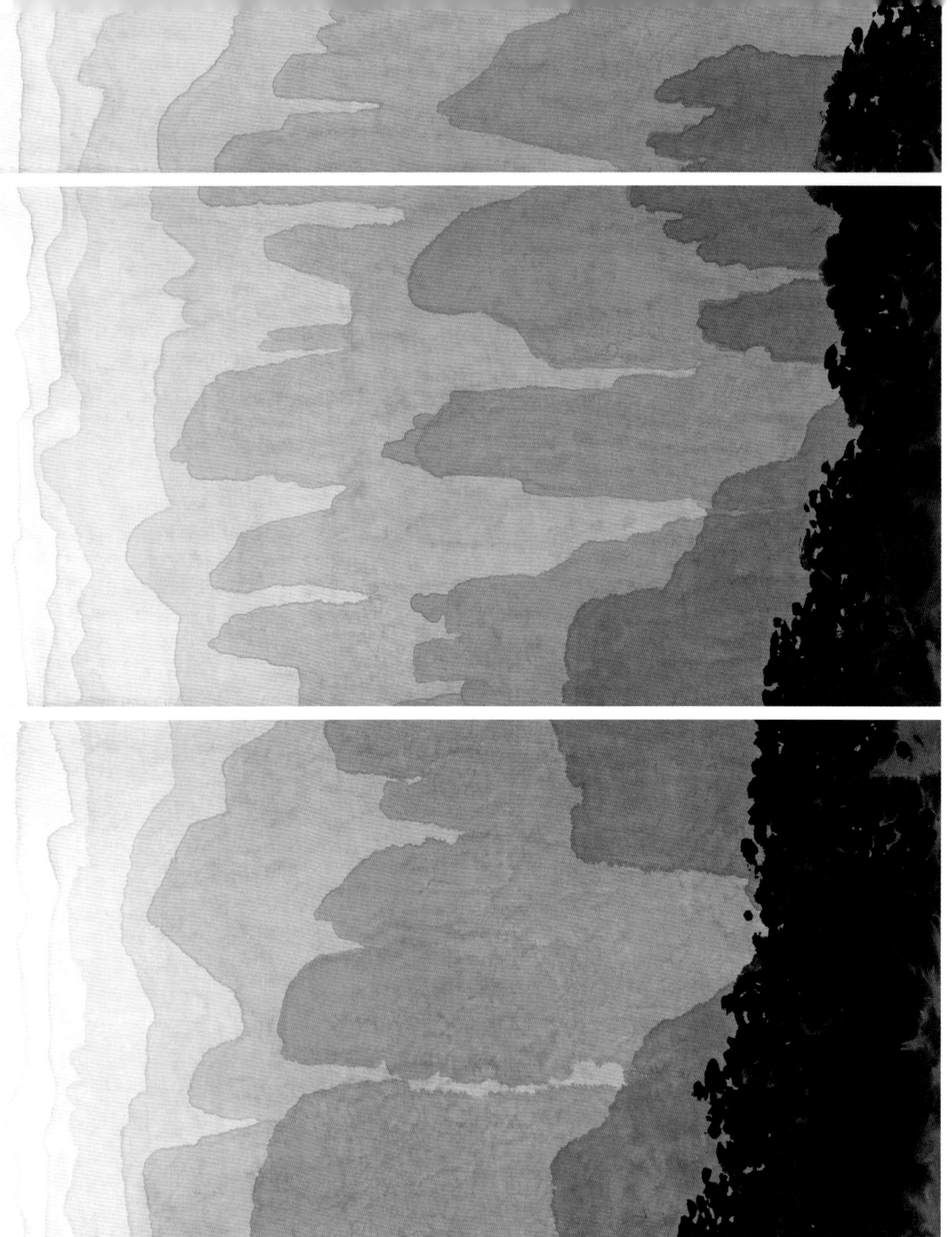

陈家泠 《黄山》 200cm×100cm×5 2009年 中国国家博物馆藏
Mount Huangshan by Chen Jialing 200cm×100cm×5 2009 National Museum of China

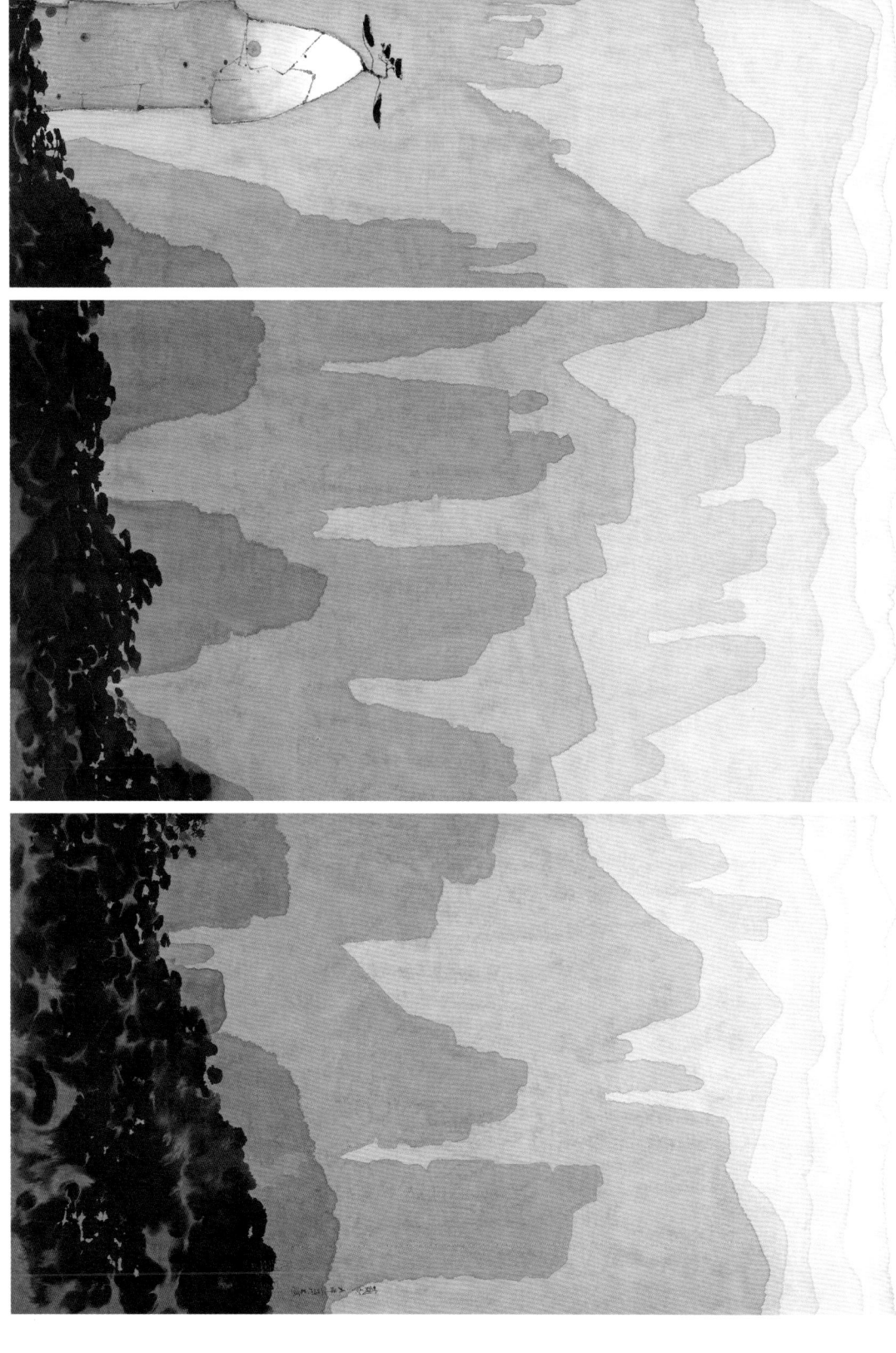

2012年冬，拍摄《陈家泠》纪录片实景，满山的雾松壮观至至极
The scene of shooting the documentary film *Chen Jialing* in the winter of 2012.
Rime scattering over the hills and dales formed a real spectacle

Rime is neither ice nor snow. It is common in the north in winter, but very rare in Mount Huangshan, not to mention the spectacle of rime scattering over the hills and dales. When the documentary film *Chen Jialing* was shot, it happened to be the best season of rime. I think this was nature's reward for Chen Jialing who has devoted a lifetime to praising nature and depicting the magnificence of natural landscape.

雾凇非冰非雪。在北方冬季常见的雾凇,而在黄山却十分难得一见,更何况是漫山遍野的雾凇奇观。在《陈家泠》纪录片拍摄时,正好遇上绝佳的雾凇场景,我想这就是大自然对陈家泠一生赞美自然、书写大美河山的回馈吧。

陈家泠的"精、气、神"
Chen Jialing's "Energy and spirit"

This is a group of close-ups when Chen Jialing was sketching. It is not hard to see how focused he was when he was collecting materials and sketching in different places, at different seasons and on different occasions.

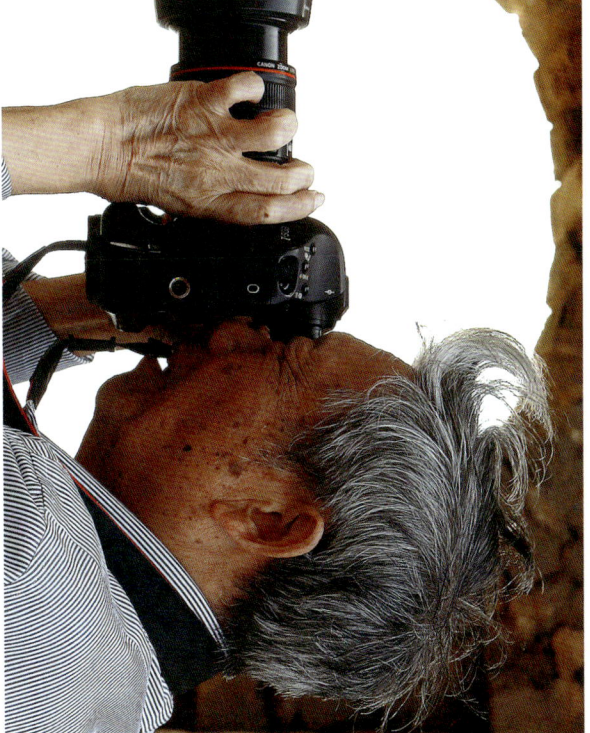
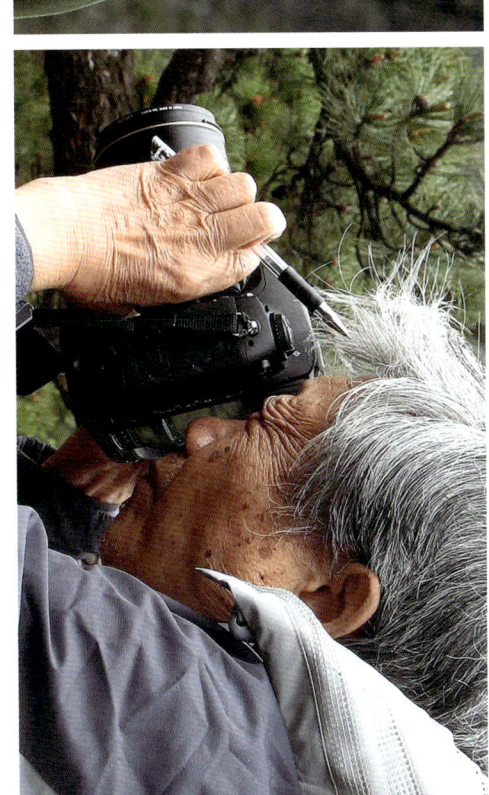

这是一组陈家泠写生的特写照,不难看出陈家泠在不同地方、不同季节、不同场合收集资料与写生时的高专注度。

陈家泠在"三山五岳"中为艺术而攀登
Chen Jialing climbed onto the top of China's famous mountains to collect materials for artistic creation

Known as Nanyue (the Southern Mountain), Mount Hengshan is one of the five famous mountains in China. Zhurong Peak, the highest peak of the 72 peaks, is located within Nanyue District, Hengyang City, Hunan Province. The towering peaks are in marked contrast to the surrounding plains and seem to reach into the clouds. The mountain peaks are covered with verdure and the trees of all sorts are vying for glamour. Springs and waterfalls present a charming sight. The scenery varies from season to season: blooming flowers in spring, the sea of clouds in summer, the sunrise in autumn and the snow in winter. The scenery also varies from spot to spot: The loftiness of Zhurong Peak, the delicacy of Tripitaka Temple, the quietness of Fangguang Temple and the mystery of Water-screen Cave are the four wonders renowned since ancient time.

陈家泠 《南岳》（五岳之衡山） 200cm×100cm×5 2011年
Nanyue (Mount Hengshan, the Southern Mountain of the five famous mountains in China) by Chen Jialing 200cm×100cm×5 2011

南岳衡山为中华五岳名山之一，有七十二峰，主峰祝融峰在湖南省衡阳市南岳区境内，这里风光秀美，群峰逶迤，其势如飞。置身其中，感受具群峰叠翠，万木争荣，流泉飞瀑，风景绮丽的自然美景，攀援的艰辛之感顿消。衡山的美不在一时而在四时，四时的景色各异，春赏奇花，夏观云海，秋望日出，冬赏雪景。衡山的美不在一处而在处处，祝融峰之高，藏经殿之秀，方广寺之深，水帘洞之奇，自古被赞誉为南岳"四绝"。

陈家泠为祝融峰祝融寺书写门联
Chen Jialing wrote door couplets for Zhurong Temple

2011年11月，陈家泠由嵩山少林寺延林法师陪同在少室山的景凉峭壁上收集创作素材

In Nov. 2011, accompanied by the senior Buddhist monk Yanlin of Shaolin Temple, Chen Jialing climbed onto the cliffs of Shaoshi Mountain to collect materials for creation

Located in Dengfeng City, Henan Province, Mount Songshan is composed of Taishi Mountain and Shaoshi Mountain. The lowest point is 350 meters and highest is 1,512 meters above sea level.

Shaoshi Mountain, also known as "Nine-summit lotus mountain", has 36 peaks which are steep and precipitous forming a peculiar and enchanting view. There are 40-odd scenic spots here like "Monkeys Watching the Sea of Clouds", "Autumn in Shaoshi Mountain", "Howling Tiger Cloud Peak", "Three-Fairy Stone", "Stalagmites Playing in the Forest", "Snow in Shaoshi Mountain", "Trayastrimsa Pond", "Tea Fairy Spring", "Human Ancestor Stone", "Shaoshi Temple", "Shaolin Temple", "Yonghua Hall of Shaolin", etc. The main peak of Shaoshi Mountain is the highest in Mount Songshan. Shaolin Temple is tucked away amid the dense woods of Mount Songshan, hence the name "Shaolin Temple in Mount Songshan".

嵩山位于河南省登封市，主要山脉是太室山与少室山，海拔最低处为350米，最高处为1512米。少室山，又名"九顶莲花山"，少室山的三十六峰山势陡峭嶙峋，奇峰异观，有猴子观云海、少室秋色、云峰虎啸、三仙石、石笋闹林、少室晴雪、切利天池、玉仙泉、人祖石、少室寺、少林寺、少林永化堂等景点40余处。少室山的主峰连天峰，为嵩山最高峰，少林寺位于其中，故名"嵩山少林寺"。

陈家泠 《中岳》（五岳之嵩山） 200cm×100cm×5 2011年
上海玉佛禅寺陈家泠佛教艺术馆藏

Zhongyue (Mount Songshan, the Central Mountain of the Five Famous Mountains in China) by Chen Jialing 200cm×100cm×5 2011 Chen Jialing Buddhist Art Hall of Shanghai Jade Buddha Temple

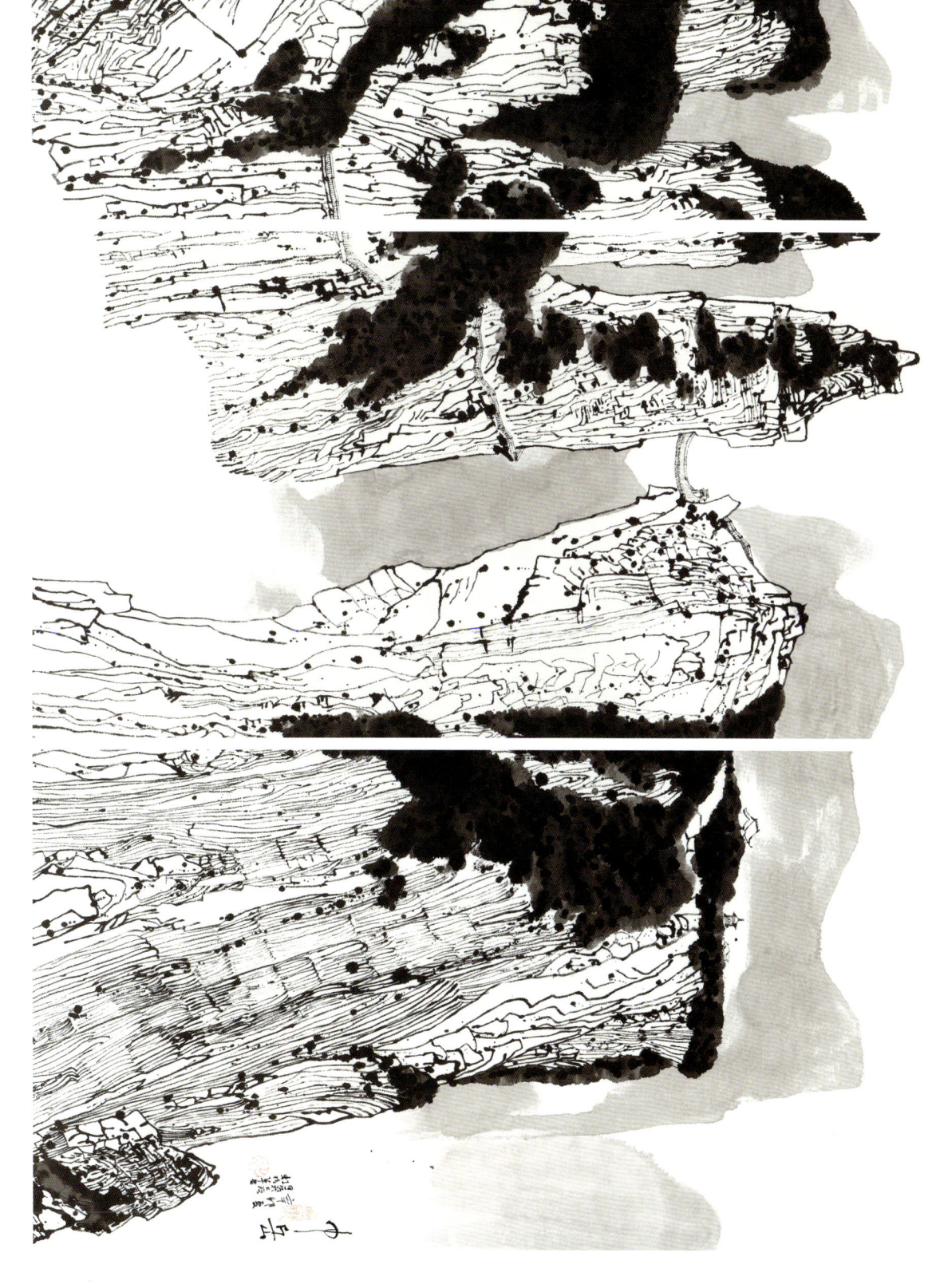

峨眉山金顶"佛光"中显现出我们虚幻的身影
Our illusory figures appeared in the distant "Light of Buddha" on the Gold Peak of Mount Emei

On Mar. 11, 2011, fog shrouded the scenic spot of Mount Emei in Sichuan Province with a visibility of only 20 meters. We prayed silently at the foot of the mountain for the fog to lift. Luckily, our prayers were answered. When our cable car rose to two-thirds of the height, suddenly it jumped out of the thick clouds. As far as our eyes could see, a sea of clouds was all around. When Chen Jialing climbed onto the Gold Peak, the clouds broke away, the sun rose up, and "Light of Buddha" in the distance emerged in the sea of clouds. We waved our hands in salute to the wonder, and our illusory figures appeared in the distant "Light of Buddha". Everything changed in an instant; our hearts were filled with good wishes inexplicably. We waved and shouted to the wonder, we saluted nature with awe. For a long time, our figures were still visible in the distant mountain, perhaps this is what is meant by "Sincerity can work wonders."

2011年3月11日，浓雾笼罩下，四川峨眉山景区的能见度仅20米，我们在山脚下默默地祈祷云雾尽快散去。果不其然，当我们乘坐的缆车上升到三分之二的高度时，忽然间缆车窜出厚厚的云层，极目望去，四周一片云海。当陈家冷冷登上金顶后，只见云开日出，远处的"佛光"在云海中出现。

我们拜手向奇观呼唤致敬，远处的"佛光"中显现出我们虚幻的身影，一切的变化都在瞬间，我们心中充满了一种莫名的祥愿。我们拜手向奇观呼唤，我们以敬畏之心向自然致敬，久久地，我们的身影仍显现在远山之中，也许这就是心诚则灵吧。

陈家泠在峨眉山顶极目浩瀚无垠的云海
Chen Jialing looked at the vast sea of clouds at the top of Mount Emei

This is the miraculous "Light of Buddha" phenomenon in Mount Emei, Sichuan Province, but more miracles were yet to come. When we looked to the east from the Gold Peak of Mount Emei, we saw the sea of clouds surging up, even the staff on the mountain marveled at the rarity of such a scene. After stopping for a moment at the Golden Peak, we resumed our journey. When finding the ideal angle, Chen Jialing started recording the scenery with his camera and sketchbook.

峨眉山神奇美妙的云雾
The magic, wonderful clouds on Mount Emei

这就是四川峨眉山神奇的"佛光"现象。奇迹还在后面，当我们从峨眉金顶在向东看去，这时风起云舞，云海涌动了起来，就连山上的工作人员都感叹此情此景很难见到。在金顶停留片刻后我们又继续赶路，当找到理想的角度后，陈家冷便用照相机和写生薄不停地记录起来……

陈家泠 《峨眉山》（中国佛教圣地之一） 200cm×100cm×5 2011年
上海玉佛禅寺陈家泠佛教艺术馆藏
Mount Emei (One of China's Buddhist shrines) by Chen Jialing 200cm×100cm×5 2011
Chen Jialing Buddhist Art Hall of Shanghai Jade Buddha Temple

峨眉烟云
Smoke and clouds on Mount Emei

陈家泠在九华山悬崖边上写生，年轻人想着他写生的画面，都要小心翼翼地扶着石墩
Chen Jialing sketched at the cliffside in Mount Jiuhua. Young people who wanted to see his sketches had to come forward by gripping the stone pier carefully

Mount Jiuhua is one of the four Buddhist mountains in China. Famous for its Earth Store Bodhisattva Dojo all over the world, pilgrims have flocked to the mountain for thousands of years. Li Bai, a famous poet in the Tang Danasty wrote down the famous lines when he visited the mountain, originally known as Mount Jiuhua: "The mystery of Yin and yang permeates /The beauty of nine flowers prevails." Known to have 99 peaks, Mount Jiuhua looks like a lotus flower in full bloom from a distance, hence the name "A Lotus World of Buddhists".

188

陈家泠《九华山》(中国佛教圣地之一) 200cm×100cm×5 2011年
上海玉佛禅寺陈家泠佛教艺术馆藏
Mount Jiuhua (one of the Buddhist shrines in China) by Chen Jialing 200cm×100cm×5 2011
Chen Jialing Buddhist Art Hall of Shanghai Jade Buddha Temple

九华山是我国四大佛教名山之一，以地藏菩萨道场名闻天下，千百年来香火旺盛。九华山古名九子山，唐代诗人李白游九华山曾留下著名诗句："妙有分二气，灵山开九华。"九华山素有九十九峰之称，远看像一朵盛开的莲花，也因此有"莲花佛国"之称。

陈家泠2011年5月16日在山西晋祠、5月18日在天台山和6月2日在山东泰安嵌寨创作集创作素材

Chen Jialing visited Jinci Temple, Shanxi Province on May 16, 2011, Mount Tiantai in Sichuan Province on May 18 and Tai'an City in Shangdong Province on Jun.2 to collect materials for creation

In Nov. 2011, "Free Roaming in China's Famous Mountains" — An Exhibition of Chen Jialing's Artworks was held at Anhui Provincial Museum. Those who viewed the exhibition shared the same feeling: Chen Jialing used painting to write about this era with extraordinary perseverance, tenacity and resolution.

Everywhere he went, Chen Jialing would make an in-depth study and judgment of the environment through inquiry and observation. He would choose the best angle for sketching and photographing to collect rich materials for creation. Every detail and form of beauty was carefully noted in his sketches. He was a painter as well as a photographer, and his photographs were better than movies.

2011年11月，"神游·三山五岳四圣"——陈家泠作品展在安徽省博物馆举办，凡是看过展览的人都有同样的感受：陈家泠以过人的毅力，坚韧不拔的勇气，义无反顾的精神，用绘画书写时代。陈家泠每到一地，都是一看、三问、三观察，深入研判环境，选择最佳角度进行写生与摄影，充分收集创作素材。凡是美的局部细节、美的形式，他都在写生素材中做仔细备注。他既是画家，也是摄影家，他的摄影作品完美得象过大片。

陈家泠在台湾阿里山的神木洞中,从长满青草和青苔的下坡路上小心翼翼地穿过

Chen Jialing walked down a grassy and mossy slope carefully through the sacred tree cave of Ali Mountain, Taiwan

陈家泠在燕子口悬崖上写生
Chen Jialing sketched on the cliff of Swallows' Mouth

Swallows' Mouth is a canyon cliff in Taroko, Taiwan, China. About 500 meters above the canyon cliff are numerous small caves. The swallows nest in the canyon, forming the spectacle of "100 swallows singing in the canyon", hence the name "Swallows' mouth".

燕子口是我国台湾太鲁阁的一段峡谷峭壁。在约500米的峡谷峭壁上，有无数小岩洞，山谷间的燕群在其间筑巢而居，形成"百燕鸣谷"的奇景，也因此有"燕子口"之名。

陈家泠在三仙台小岛上攀登
Chen Jialing climbed onto the island of Sanxiantai (Three-Immortal Pavilion)

This is a series of shots of Chen Jialing climbing onto Sanxiantai (Three-Immortal Pavilion) Island in Taitung, Taiwan, China. I was once again struck by his spirit of scaling the heights when he climbed up the mountain and looked out over the Pacific from the top.

Located in Taitung County, Sanxiantai Island consists of a coral reef and three volcanic peaks that are triangular and dark brown. Legend has it that Iron Crutch Li, Lv Dongbin and He Xiangu of the "Eight Immortals" once rested on this island, and left three pairs of footprints on the mountain, hence the name Sanxiantai (Three-Immortal Pavilion).

这是陈家泠在我国台湾台东三仙台上攀登的一组镜头,当他爬上山头,从山顶上遥望太平洋时,我又一次被他那敢于攀登的精神所震撼。

三仙台位于台东县,岛由珊瑚礁海岸和三座火山岩山峰构成,山峰呈三角状,黑褐色。相传"八仙"中的铁拐李、吕洞宾、何仙姑曾于此岛上停憩,在山上留下三双足印,故名三仙台。

和美世界

A World of Harmony and Beauty

4

陈家泠钻进玄奘曾经打坐的洞窟
Chen Jialing crawled into the cave where Xuanzang once meditated

In Jan. 2018, Chen Jialing went to India with the artists of Shanghai Jade Buddha Temple to visit the ten ruins of Gautama Buddha. At each place, Chen Jialing would listen carefully to the guide's explanation of Gautama Buddha's history, biography, ancient buildings and classical Buddhist culture, and raise many questions. He would take careful notes in the form of photographing, and write down the time, place and feature in the form of sketching. When coming to a cave where Xuanzang once meditated in Nalanda, compared with most of the tourists who just looked at the 50cm-high and less than 50cm-wide cave entrance and listened to the guide, Chen Jialing bent down, put his head in to see the interior, looked both sides up and down, then crawled straight into the dark and narrow cave. Of course, I followed him closely behind. I saw him crouching down and sitting at the bottom of the cave which was just large enough to hold his body. At this point, Chen Jialing calmly experienced what Xuanzang was experiencing at that time, while I quickly adjusted the camera's mode under the faint light of my cell phone to record the precious image of Chen Jialing.

2018年1月，陈家泠随上海玉佛禅寺的艺术家一同前往印度，参观考察释迦牟尼十大遗址。所到之处，陈家泠都会仔细听导游对相关的历史、人物故事、古建筑和经典佛教文化场的讲解并多次提问，用照相的形式认真记录，用写生把时间、地点以及特点都一一写下来。当他来到玄奘在那烂陀寺取经打坐的一个洞窟时，绝大多数参观旅游者只是望着高50厘米、宽不到50厘米的洞口听导游讲解，而陈家泠却弯下腰，把头探到洞窟内，四面上下打量了一下，便直接钻进了既暗又狭小的洞中了。当然我也紧跟了进去，只见陈家泠已蹲伏着坐到了洞窟的底部，而底部的空间恰好容下他的全身。此时陈家泠静静地体悟玄奘当年的情形，而我则用手机微弱的光，迅速地调整好拍摄模式，记录下陈家泠此时最珍贵的影像。

恒河边上的印度民众
Indian people by the Ganges

The Ganges is revered by the Indian people as the "Sacred river" and "Mother of India". Numerous myths and religious legends constitute the unique customs of the Ganges. Indians believe in bathing in the Ganges at least once in a lifetime, to let the holy river cleanse their sin.

陈家泠在恒河边上,向满天飞翔的海鸥挥手致意
Chen Jialing waved to the flying seagulls by the Ganges

恒河被印度人民尊称为"圣河"和"印度的母亲"。众多的神话故事和宗教传说构成了恒河两岸独特的风土人情。印度人崇尚一生中至少要在恒河中沐浴一次,让圣河洗净罪业。

2018年1月13日，陈家泠在印度灵鹫山写生
On Jan. 13, 2018, Chen Jialing sketched in Griddhraj Parvat, India

Griddhraj Parvat in India is the place where Gautama Buddha proclaimed his teachings. *The Prajna Paramita*, *The Lotus Sutra*, *The Samantabhadra Meditation Sutra*, *The Buddhist Samadhi Sutra* and the like were all proclaimed on Griddhraj Parvat. Faxian, a Chinese monk from East Jin and Xuanzang, a Chinese monk from the Tang Dynasty, both traveled here. Xuanzang wrote of the Griddhraj Parvat landscape in *Traveling Notes of Western Lands in Great Tang Dynasty*: With the sun shining on the north hill, the whole mountain uplifts abruptly from the ground, with lofty ridges and towering peaks rising upon one another. At the top of the main peak stands a rock in the shape of a vulture's head, hence the name Griddhraj Parvat (Vulture's Peak).

印度灵鹫山是释迦牟尼宣说佛法妙义之地，如《大般若波罗蜜多经》《妙法莲华经》《无量义经》《佛说法华三昧经》等，都是在灵鹫山上宣说的。中国东晋高僧法显和唐朝高僧玄奘都曾云游到此。玄奘在《大唐西域记》中描写灵鹫山的景色时就写道："接北山之阳，孤标特起，既栖鹫鸟，又类高台，空翠相映，浓淡分色。"

陈家泠在舍卫城菩提树下为僧侣写生人物肖像
Chen Jialing sketched a portrait of a monk under a Bodhi tree in Shravasti

The city of Shravasti in India is famous for its beautiful houses. Legend has it that Gautama Buddha lived here for years to proclaim his teachings. It was the capital of Kosala of ancient India, in what is now Uttar Pradesh, on the southern bank of the Lapidus.

陈家泠将抓拍的照片展示给信众看
Chen Jialing showed the snapshots to the Buddhist followers

印度的舍卫城因祇园精舍而闻名于世,相传释迦牟尼长年在此说法。它是古印度拘萨罗国都城,在今印度北方邦北部,拉普蒂河南岸。

陈家泠在印度北方邦的鹿野苑写生
Chen Jialing sketched in Sarnath in Uttar Pradesh, India

壮丽雄伟的科罗拉多大峡谷
The magnificent Grand Canyon

Grand Canyon Colorado, located on the Kaibab Plateau in northwestern Arizona, USA, is a world-famous natural wonder. In 1980, the Grand Canyon National Park where the Colorado Canyon was located was included on the World Heritage List.

In order to record and film the Grand Canyon, Chen Jialing would go to the Grand Canyon every morning to film the sunrise. During the day, except eating, he would spend all the time sketching and shooting materials for creation until the sun went down. So there were complete records of every place he went.

陈家冷俯瞰科罗拉多大峡谷壮丽雄伟的景色
Chen Jialing overlooked the magnificent scenery of the Grand Canyon

美国科罗拉多大峡谷，位于亚利桑那州西北部的凯巴布高原上，是举世闻名的自然奇观。1980年，科罗拉多大峡谷所在的大峡谷国家公园被列入世界遗产名录。

为了记录与拍摄科罗拉多大峡谷，陈家冷每天清晨就赶到大峡谷拍摄日出，白天除了吃饭外就是写生与拍摄创作素材直到太阳下山为止，所以陈家冷所到之处都有完整的记录。

2019年11月8日,陈家泠拍摄科罗拉多大峡谷壮丽雄伟的景色
Chen Jialing took photos of the magnificent Grand Canyon on Nov. 8, 2019

2019年11月8日,陈家冷拍摄科罗拉多大峡谷壮丽雄伟的景色
Chen Jialing took photos of the magnificent Grand Canyon on Nov. 8, 2019

科罗拉多河马蹄弯
Horseshoe Bend, Colorado River, USA

Horseshoe Bend is a great bend in the Colorado River, USA. The Green Colorado River goes around the red horseshoe-shaped rocks, forming a 270° bend, an "entrenched meander" as it is called. The River is often red because of the amount of sediment it carries. Approximately 300-meter vertical drops, a 270° U-shaped curve, blue sky, green water and red rocks, and a majestic natural wonder is confronting you.

马蹄湾是美国科罗拉多河上的一个大拐弯，约300米直下的悬崖，绿色的科罗拉多河围绕着红色的马蹄状岩石，蜿蜒流淌出270°的转角，因为河中夹带大量泥沙，河水常显红色。约300米的垂直落差，270°U形弯道，蓝天碧水红岩，构成气势磅礴的自然奇景。

陈家泠在去美国科罗拉多大峡谷途中随时发现并抓取、记录有创作价值的素材
On his way to the Grand Canyon in USA, Chen Jialing kept discovering and making quick notes of the valuable materials for creation

陈家泠与许根顺在美国大山深处比武练功
Chen Jialing and Xu Genshun practised martial arts in the depths of the mountain in USA

221

陈家泠在芝加哥公牛队体育礼品专卖店里做迈克尔·乔丹投篮的潇洒动作
Chen Jialing imitated a Michael Jordan shot at the Chicago Bulls' sports gift shop

Chicago Bulls is no doubt one of the most representative teams in Chicago, it is also popular with basketball fans all over the world. At the sports gift shop, one can buy jerseys bearing the names of Bulls' superstars and find caps and souvenirs with Bulls' logo.

2019年11月9日，属相都为牛的陈家伶与许根顺在芝加哥公牛队家乡的品牌店里合影
On Nov. 9, 2019, Chen Jialing and Xu Genshun, both born in the year of Ox, posed for a group photo at the Chicago Bulls home store

芝加哥公牛队无疑是芝加哥最具代表意义的球队之一，也是到全世界篮球迷的追捧。在专营体育礼品店里，人们能买到印有公牛队当红巨星形象的球衣，还能找到印有公牛队队标的帽子及小礼品。

2019年11月,陈家泠参观康宁玻璃博物馆
In Nov. 2019, Chen Jialing visited the Corning Glass Museum

The Corning Museum of Glass in USA is dedicated to the development and research of art, history and the science of glass. It now boasts more than 50,000 pieces of glassware, some of which are more than 3,500 years old. Chen Jialing is very interested in glassware. In his artistic creation, besides painting and calligraphy, he is also very keen on silk, furniture, porcelain art, purple clay, etc. One can tell his strong interest from his earnest, absorbed look at the glassware as he visited the Corning Glass Museum.

美国康宁玻璃博物馆致力于艺术、历史和玻璃科学的开发与研究。目前拥有超过50000件玻璃制品，其中一些已有3500多年的历史。对于玻璃制品，陈家泠同样十分感兴趣。在他的艺术创作中，除了绘画与书法，也对丝绸、家具、瓷艺、紫砂等十分感兴趣，从他在康宁玻璃博物馆参观玻璃器皿时的那种专心认真的神情，就不难看出他强烈的兴趣点。

陈家泠在华盛顿与爱因斯坦雕像"对话"
Chen Jialing had a "dialogue" with the statue of Einstein in Washington, DC, USA

Einstein is a great scientist. On his centennial birthday, a bronze statue of Einstein, which was nearly four meters high and weighed about four tons, was built. The Einstein in the statue has a familiar face, a deep and wise gaze. Holding a piece of paper with three mathematical equations in his left hand, he seemed to be thinking about more research topics.

In Nov. 2019, Chen Jialing had a "dialogue" with the statue of Einstein in Washington, DC, USA. This cross-century, interdisciplinary, and translocal dialogue formed a very interesting picture. The contrast of colors and sizes of the characters made the dialogue more interesting.

爱因斯坦是伟大的科学家,在其诞辰 100 周年之际,一个以铜质铸成的高近 4 米,重约 4 吨的爱因斯坦雕像落成。雕像中的爱因斯坦有着世人熟悉的面容,深邃智慧的眼神,左手拿着写有三个数学等式的纸似乎还在思考更多的研究课题。

2019 年 11 月,陈家泠在美国华盛顿与爱因斯坦雕像"对话",这一跨世纪,跨学科,跨地域的隔空对话,是一幅十分有趣的照片,具形成的色彩鲜明对比,人物大小对比,更加突出了对话的趣味性。

陈家泠在黄石国家公园
Chen Jialing was in the Yellowstone National Park

The Yellowstone National Park mainly lies in the northwest corner of Wyoming in mid-western United States, and stretches northwest to Idaho and Montana. Established in 1872, t is the world's first national park, and was listed as a world natural heritage in 1978. It is a truly extraordinary spectacle featuring an abundance of rivers, lakes, streams, springs, ponds, and waterfalls, etc.

In Nov. 2019, Chen Jialing toured around the Yellowstone National Park as the last batch of visitors before winter and the last batch to leave it. In the Park, Chen Jialing took care to visit all the scenic spots, sketched and photographed a large number of snow scenes and geothermal wonders.

美国黄石国家公园主要位于美国中西部怀俄明州的西北角，并向西北方向延伸到爱达荷州和蒙大拿州，成立于1872年，1978年被列为世界自然遗产，是世界第一座国家公园。公园内河、湖、溪、泉、塘、大小瀑布，应有尽有，勾画出一幅梦幻迷人的景色。

2019年11月，陈家冷是黄石公园冬季来临前最后一批进园的游客，也是最后一批出园的游客。在黄石公园，陈家冷十分认真地游览了园内的各个景点，写生并拍摄了大量雪景与地热奇观。

陈家泠在羚羊峡谷中拍摄鬼斧神工的自然界奇观
Chen Jialing photographed the uncanny natural wonder in Antelope Canyon

Antelope Canyon of us is one of the famous slot canyons in the world. It is so named presumably because it is frequented by pronghorn antelopes.

The light in the passageways in Antelope Canyon varies. Only during a short period of time at noon does the sun reach the canyon floor through a few cracks. The rock composition here is known as red sandstone, and the rocks in the canyon are washed away by torrential floods, presenting a striking and mesmerizing beauty.

美国羚羊峡谷是世界上著名的狭缝型峡谷之一。据说这里因是叉角羚羊经常光顾的地方而得名。羚羊峡谷通道的光线千变万化，只有在正午很短的一段时间里阳光才能透过几处间隙照到谷底。这里的岩石是著名的红砂岩，谷内岩石被山洪冲刷成了梦幻世界。

陈家泠在盐湖城山区的沙地上，拍摄侧光照射下的一个个有趣的脚印
Chen Jialing took photos of interesting footprints formed under the sidelight in the sands of the mountain area of Salt Lake City

Salt Lake City is the capital and largest city of Utah, USA, named for its proximity to Great Salt Lake.

盐湖城是美国犹他州首府和最大城市,以紧靠大盐湖而得名。

陈家泠在日本樱花节期间写生
Chen Jialing sketched during the Cherry Blossom Festival in Japan

In the spring of 2012, during the Japanese Cherry Blossom Festival, Chen Jialing went to Japan to shoot the documentary *Chen Jialing* with Shanghai Film Studios.

2012年春,陈家泠在日本樱花节期间,随上海电影制片厂进行纪录片《陈家泠》的拍摄。

陈家泠在日本奈良的寺庙写生
Chen Jialing sketched at a temple in Nara, Japan

陈家泠在日本新干线,途中利用候车时间用餐
Chen Jialing had his meal while waiting for the Shinkansen train

空中俯瞰乌鲁鲁全景
A panoramic view of Uluru from above

The Midwest of Australia is a desolate moor with little rain. The temperature is high around noon and the difference between morning and evening is great. Uluru-Katachutta National Park is a world famous tourist attraction in the center of Australia, which consists of two parts: uluru, also known as Ayers Rock, and Kata Tjuta. Uluru is the largest single rock in the world, known as "the red heart of Australia", located in South Katachutta National Park of the Northern Territory in the center of Australia. Uluru refers to a single red rock of 349 meters high and nearly 10 kilometers in circumference.

In Mar. 6, 2019, Chen Jialing came to Australia and made a special trip to Uluru. The local temperature was high and there was little rain, one could only be outdoors in the early morning and in the late afternoon. That day, Chen Jialing drove to Uluru before dawn to watch the sunrise and sketch.

清晨的第一缕阳光照在乌鲁鲁火红的巨石山体上
The first rays of the morning sun hit the huge, red Boulder Mountains of Uluru

澳大利亚的中西部是荒无人烟的沙漠，干旱少雨，中午前后气温高，早晚温差大。位于澳大利亚大陆中央的乌鲁鲁-卡塔丘塔国家公园是世界著名的旅游胜地，其由两部分组成：乌鲁鲁（Uluru，也称艾尔斯岩 Ayers Rock）和卡塔丘塔（Kata Tjuta）。乌鲁鲁是世界最大的单体岩石，有"澳大利亚的红色心脏"之称。

2019年3月6日，陈家冷来到澳大利亚并专程前往乌鲁鲁，当地气温高而且干旱少雨，一般只能清晨与傍晚前在野外活动。当天，陈家冷天不亮就驱车赶往乌鲁鲁看日出并写生。

为了避开强烈的阳光,陈家泠选择在一块巨石阴影下写生
In order to avoid strong sunlight, Chen Jialing chose a large stone and sketched under its shadow

陈家泠在澳大利亚乌鲁鲁戴着网罩写生
Chen Jialing sketched in Uluru, Australia wearing a specially made net

The fly in Uluru, Australia is famous for being as small as a sesame but as strong as a bull fly. Like a mosquito, it is silent, dense and flexible. It particularly likes to get into people's eyes, nostrils, and ears, and can not be driven away. So when going out, one has to cover his/her head with a specially made net.

澳大利亚鲁鲁的苍蝇是有名的，小如芝麻，劲如牛蝇，似蚊虫悄无声息，密度高且灵活性大，它特别喜欢往人的眼睛、鼻孔、耳朵里钻，而且赶都赶不走，所以外出时头部就必须戴好专制的网罩。

陈家泠在澳大利亚写生
Chen Jialing sketched in Australia

2019年春，陈家泠在澳大利亚海边欣赏风光
In the spring of 2019, Chen Jialing enjoyed the scenery on the coast of Australia

The Twelve Apostles on the southern coast of Australia lies in the Port Campbell National Park on Ocean Road. The Twelve Apostles is actually a rock standing in the ocean. Originally part of a coastline, it gradually broke away after being eroded by surging waves and high winds. It is so called because these twelve pillars bring to mind the Twelve Apostles who followed Jesus Christ in the *Bible*.

澳大利亚南部海岸的十二使徒岩,位于大洋路上的坎贝尔港国家公园内。十二使徒岩其实就是屹立在海中的岩石,最初是海岸线的一部分,经过海浪和大风的侵蚀,逐渐脱离开来。因为这十二根石柱让人联想到《圣经》故事中追随耶稣的十二使徒,故得名"十二使徒岩"。

奥地利丰富多彩的建筑颜色
Austria's rich colors of architecture

In the summer of 2018, Chen Jialing went to Europe to sketch, during this time he visited Austria, France, Germany, Italy and other countries.

2018年夏天,陈家泠赴欧洲写生,其间他到过奥地利、法国、德国、意大利等国家。

陈家泠在东欧山区写生。雷雨即将来临之时,他一边打着雨伞一边抓紧把写生完成

Chen Jialing sketched in the mountain areas of Eastern Europe. Sensing the coming thunderstorm, he hastened to finish the sketching while holding his umbrella

陈家泠在欧洲艺术馆
Chen Jialing was in the European Museum of Art

陈家泠在欧洲艺术大馆
Chen Jialing was in the European Museum of Art

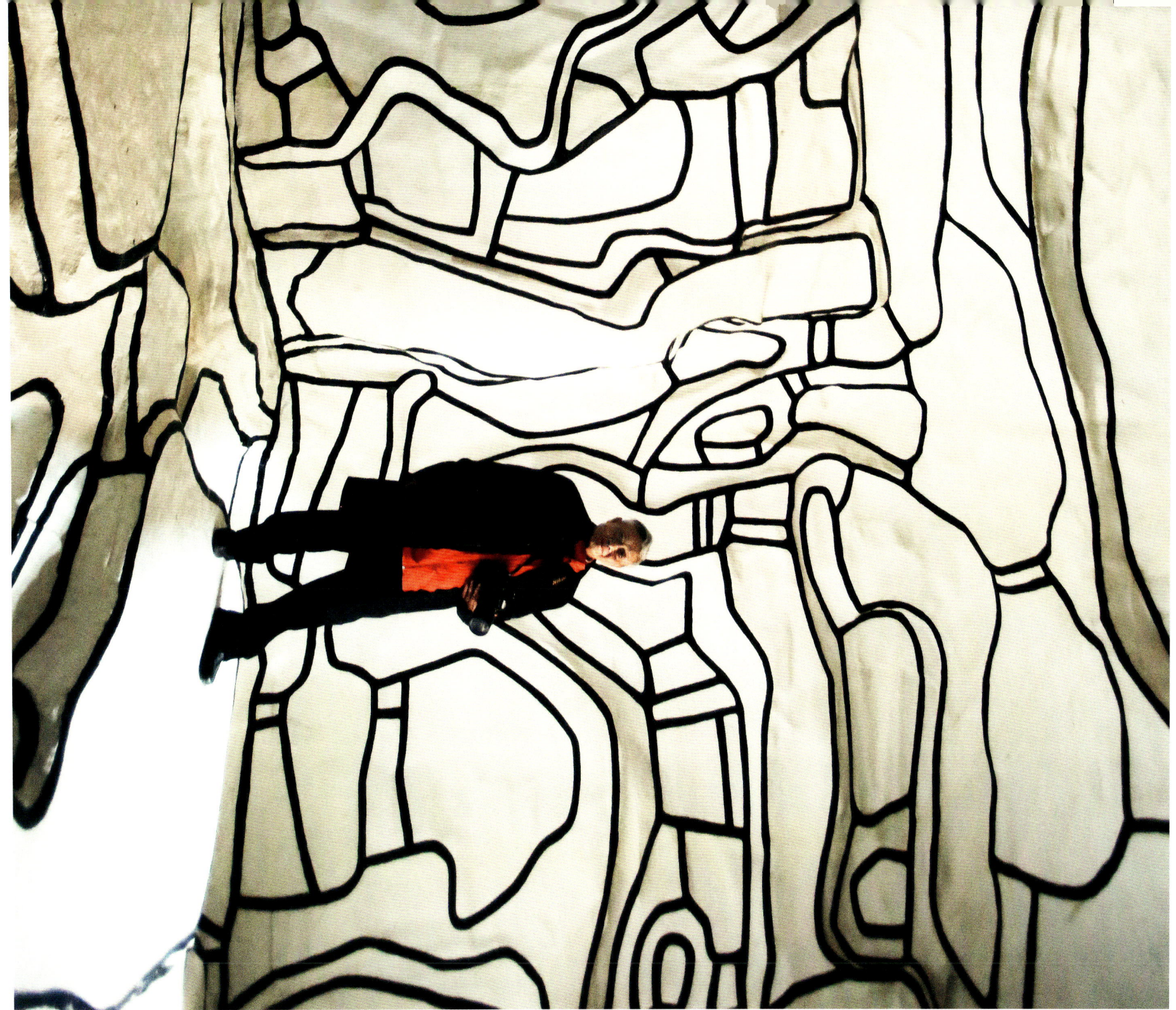

陈家泠在法国蓬皮杜美术馆
Chen Jialing was in the Pompidou Art Museum in France

陈家泠在欧洲小镇写生
Chen Jialing sketched in a small town in Europe

陈家泠在欧洲小镇写生
Chen Jialing sketched in a small town in Europe

德国巴伐利亚新天鹅堡
Schloss Neuschwanstein, Bavaria, Germany

陈家泠在德国巴伐利亚大山中写生并摄影
Chen Jialing sketched and photographed in the mountains of Kehlsteinhaus in Germany

Kehlsteinhaus lies in the Alps near Berchtesgaden, Bavaria in southern Germany, with an altitude of 1,881 meters above sea level.

鹰巢位于德国南部巴伐利亚州贝希特斯加登附近的阿尔卑斯山脉,海拔1881米。

陈家泠在德国巢穴的国王湖
Chen Jialing was in Koenigsee of Kehlsteinhaus in Germany

陈家泠在少女峰向其致以最崇高的敬意
Chen Jialing paid highest respect to Jungfrau

In autumn, 2014, after attending the "Honor screening" of the documentary *Chen Jialing* in the Ninth International Film Festival in Rome, Chen Jialing went to explore the famous Jungfrau in Switzerland. With an altitude of 4,158 meters above sea level, Jungfrau is a section of the Alps range in Bern. On that day, we took a small train to enjoy the beautiful mountains and rivers, folk residences and farms of Switzerland along the way, but Chen Jialing was busy photographing the cultural landscapes inside and outside the train. The train wound its way up the 4,000-meter mountain, then the cable car took us to its top, and Jungfrau was right before us. Chen Jialing raised both arms in front of Jungfrau to pay his highest respect.

2014年秋，陈家泠参加完纪录片《陈家泠》在第九届罗马国际电影节"荣誉放映"后，赴瑞士并登上了著名的少女峰。少女峰海拔4158米，是伯尔尼阿尔卑斯山的一部分。当天，我们一行乘坐小火车沿途欣赏瑞士美丽的山川风景、民居农场，而陈家泠却在不停地拍摄着列车内外的人文景观。火车沿着蜿蜒的山路到达少女峰，山上缆车将我们送到4000米的山顶，少女峰就在眼前。陈家泠在山峰前做了一个高高举起双臂的动作，向少女峰致以最崇高的敬意。

陈家泠在夏威夷与鹦鹉合影
Chen Jialing took a photo with parrots in Hawaii

In Nov. 2015, the documentary *Chen Jialing* won Documentary Award and Cultural Ambassador Title in the ninth International Film Festival held in Hawaii, USA. Meanwhile, accompanied by his friends, Chen Jialing visited the botanical garden, the zoological garden, the volcanic island, etc. in Hawaii. In the bird section of the zoo, Chen Jialing took a photo with parrots. The feathers of three interesting parrots were red, green and blue (three primary colors in nature) and different shades of black, white and gray. In comparison, Chen Jialing's paintings are far more colorful and gorgeous.

2015年11月,纪录片《陈家泠》在美国夏威夷第九届国际电影节上荣获纪录片大奖及文化大使奖。其间,陈家泠在朋友的陪同下,游览了夏威夷的植物园、动物园及火山岛等。在动物园的鸟类区,陈家泠与鹦鹉合影,三只有趣的鹦鹉身上的羽毛具有自然界的三原色(红、绿、蓝)与黑、白、灰三个不同的明度,而陈家泠的绘画色彩却是变化无穷,绚丽多彩的。

2013年,陈家泠在巴西枝杆稠密、河道狭窄的红树林中探秘
In 2013, Chen Jialing explored the mangroves with dense branches and narrow streamways in Brazil

Mangroves are tropical trees or shrubs along the seacoast consisting of salt-tolerant mangrove flora. Mangroves are distributed on intertidal mudflats of low-lying coastal deposits. They are most easy to develop and grow in leeward estuaries, bays and lagoons behind sandbars.

红树林由耐盐的红树林植物群落构成。红树林分布在低平的堆积海岸的潮间带泥滩上，特别在背风浪的河口、海湾与沙坝后侧的潟湖内最容易发育生长。

2017年秋，陈家泠在锡吉里耶狮子岩大山岩壁上写生
In autumn 2017, Chen Jialing sketched on the rock wall of Sigiriya Lion Rock

Sri Lanka is an enchanting island country. On this mysterious land stands a huge stone. Seen from afar, it looks like a magnificent castle, and its top faintly reveals the broken walls of man-made buildings. This is the famous Sigiriya Lion Rock. This tall and imposing monument has a long history, and is a world-class heritage under the protection of UNESCO.

斯里兰卡狮子岩大山岩壁上的壁画
The wall painting on the wall of Lion Rock in Sri Lanka

斯里兰卡是一个令人神往的美丽岛屿国家,在这具有神秘色彩的大地上,耸立着一块巨石,从远处眺望,其宛若一座雄伟的城堡,其顶部隐隐约约显露出人工建筑物的断墙残壁,这就是著名的锡吉里耶狮子岩。这个高大雄伟的古迹有着悠久历史,是受到联合国教科文组织保护的世界级珍贵遗产之一。

陈家泠在斯里兰卡当地人的护送下登上古城遗址,并在左右护卫、亲友簇拥前抓紧时间找好角度写生

Escorted by Sri Lankan locals, Chen Jialing climbed to the top of the ruins of the ancient city. Under their protection, he found a good angle for sketching promptly before the night fell

陈家泠在锡吉里耶狮子岩修葺显露的古建筑遗址上感慨异国历史的辉煌
Chen Jialing marveled at the glorious foreign history on the ruins of ancient buildings looming over Sigiriya Lion Rock

2017年春,陈家泠赴婆罗浮屠写生
In spring 2017, Chen Jialing went to the Borobudur for sketching

Borobudur Pagoda is located in the village of Borobudur in Central Java Island, Indonesia. This well-designed stone pagoda was built around 800 AD, using nearly 2,250,000 rocks. The ground floor is paved with huge stones, each weighing about one ton, and totaling 550,000 cubic meters. The bottom of the pagoda is a square, with a circumference of about 120 meters, and an altar of nine layers decorated with thousands of carvings reflecting the life of the Buddha. 72 bell-shaped pagodas or shrines stand on the circular platform, and Buddhists climb onto the Borobudur by a special route. Entering from the east, turning around clockwise, and walking to the top of the temple, this series of moves symbolizes one's gradual attainment of spiritual perfection.

婆罗浮屠塔位于印度尼西亚爪哇岛中部婆罗浮屠村,建于约公元800年。在建造时,用了近225万块岩石,底层用每块重约1吨的巨石铺就,总体积达5.5万立方米。塔底呈正方形,周长约120米,坛共有9层,装饰着数以千计的反映佛陀生活的雕刻。圆形平台上面竖立着72座钟形佛塔或佛龛,佛教徒按特定的路线登婆罗浮屠塔。从东进入,按顺时针方向绕行,走向庙顶象征着一个人逐步达到完美的精神境界。

2017年春，陈家泠在婆罗浮屠逐层认真观赏并收集创作资料

In spring 2017, Chen Jialing took a close look at the Borobudur from layer to layer and collected materials for creation

2017年春，陈家泠顶着烈阳在婆罗浮屠的圆形平台上写生

In spring 2017, Chen Jialing sketched on the circular platform of the Borobudur under the scorching sun

2017年春，陈家泠在婆罗浮屠写生
In spring 2017, Chen Jialing sketched at the Borobudur

陈家泠在皮兰古城的城墙上写生
Chen Jialing sketched on the walls of the ancient town of Piran

The town of Piran, in the south-west of Slovenia, sticks out like a bud into the middle of the sea. This is an old medieval seaside town. Narrow streets stretch from the top of the hill to the bottom, the dense buildings around the central square teeming with Mediterranean characteristics.

斯洛文尼亚西南边的皮兰小镇
Piran, a small town in Slovenia

斯洛文尼亚西南边的皮兰小镇，如同一枝花蕾探入了海中央。这是座古老的中世纪海边小镇。狭窄的街道从山上延伸到山下，中央广场周围密集的建筑充满着浓浓的地中海特色。

艺术创作
Artistic Creation

05

2021年1月30日，上海大学党委书记成旦红在上海梅龙镇艺术中心，夫心陈家泠创作生活

On Jan.30, 2021, Cheng Danhong, the Party Secretary of Shanghai University, visited Chen Jialing and enquired about his creative life at Meilong Guanyuan Art Center, Shanghai

2023年3月5日,上海大学党委书记成旦红在党委委员财务总监苟燕南的陪同下,在陈家泠在江西景德镇望龙瓷厂国家重器的创作
On Mar.5, 2023, accompanied by Gou Yannan, finance director of the party committee, Cheng Danhong, the Party Secretary of Shanghai University visited Chen Jialing and enquired about his progress on vat creation, a national treasure, in Jingdezhen Wanglong Porcelain Factory, Jiangxi province.

陈家泠讲座写生示范场景
The scene of lecture-giving and sketch demonstration by Chen Jialing

Chen Jialing delivered art lectures at Shanghai Academy of Fine Arts, Shanghai University, and gave live demonstration of figure painting to the students and teachers during the break.

陈家泠在上海大学上海美术学院作艺术讲座,课间为师生们进行人物画写生示范。

陈家泠在安徽省博物馆巨石前留影
Chen Jialing posed for a photo in front of the huge rock in Anhui Provincial Museum

In autumn 2011, Chen Jialing held a large-scale solo exhibition of his paintings entitled "Free Roaming in China's Famous Mountains" — An Exhibition of Chen Jialing's Artworks at Anhui Provincial Museum. Inside Anhui Provincial Museum there is a huge rock with a unique shape, engraved on it is a remark made by Mao Zedong when he visited the museum on Sep.17, 1958: "Every major city in a province should have a museum like this, because it is critically important that people know about their own history and creative power."

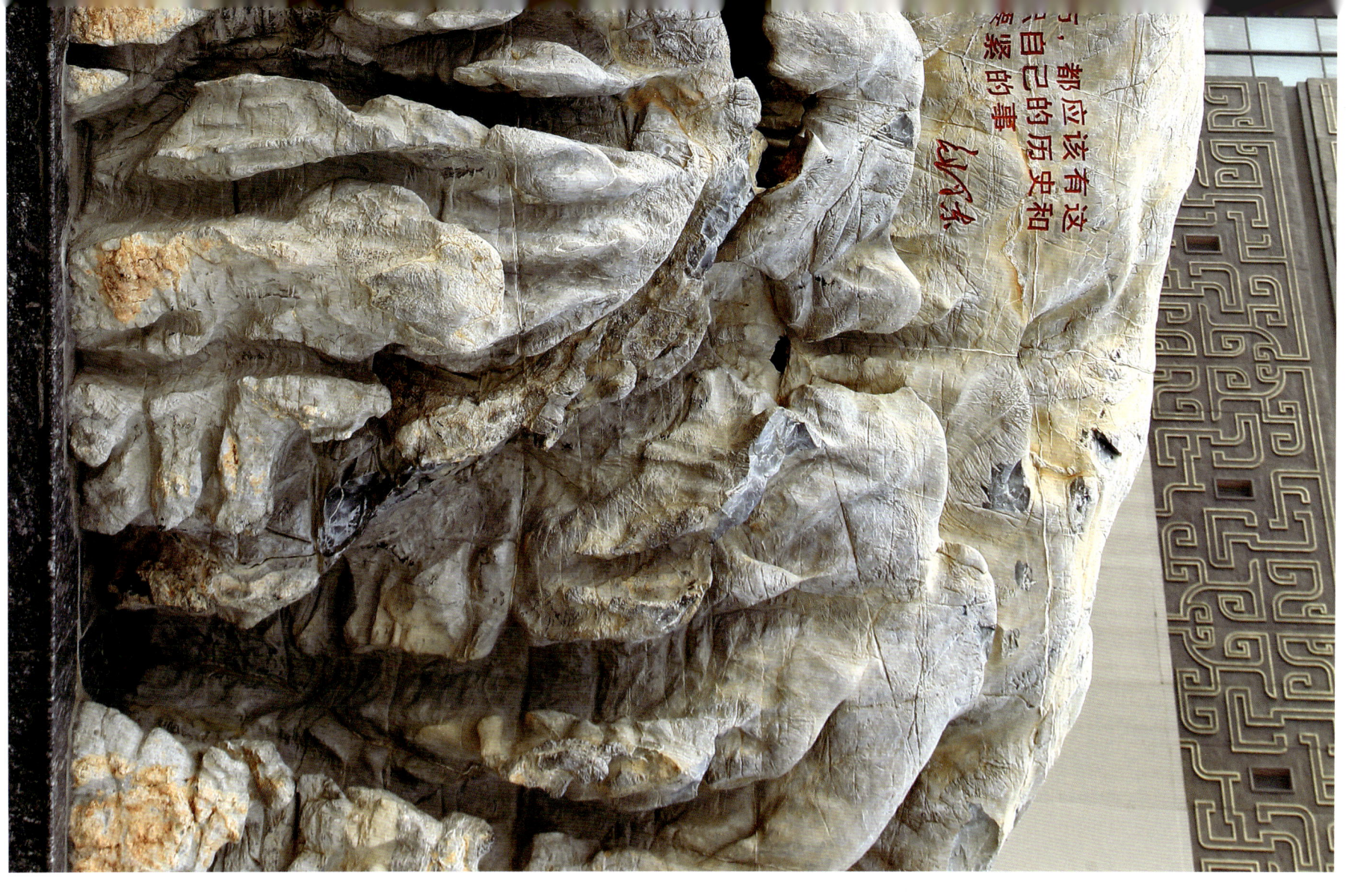

2011年秋，陈家泠在安徽省博物馆举办"神游——三山五岳四圣地"大型个人画展。安徽省博物馆内有一块造型独特的巨石，上面镌刻着1958年9月17日毛泽东视察博物馆时所写的一句话："一个省的主要城市，都应该有这样的博物馆，人民认识自己的历史和创造的力量是一件很要紧的事。"

陈家泠在陆俨少影像前留影
Chen Jialing posed for a photo in front of Lu Yanshao's projected image

Chen Jialing fondly recalled what his mentor Lu Yanshao had taught him in the studio of the documentary *Chen Jialing*.

The first reason why Chen Jialing decided to enter Hangzhou High School back then was that it had a large number of masters and scholars like Master Hong Yi, Lu Xun, Feng Zikai, and Pan Tianshou, etc. Thanks to his hard work, he was finally admitted to his dream school. During his study there, these seniors became his role model. The First Normal School of Zhejiang Province (today's Hangzhou High School) is one of the six earliest famous normal schools in China. Its predecessor was Zhejiang Two-level Normal School founded in 1908, whose reputation was evident in the saying "There is Beijing Normal School in the north, and Zhejiang First Normal School in the south".

In 1958, Chen Jialing was admitted to Zhejiang Academy of Fine Arts (today's China Academy of Fine Arts), whose dean was Pan Tianshou at that time. When he was studying there, he was deeply inspired by the dean's academic ideas and classical thoughts of Chinese painting, and regarded these ideas and thoughts as the highest goal of his life.

陈家冷在潘天寿影像前留影
Chen Jialing posed for a photo in front of Pan Tianshou's projected image

陈家冷曾经在纪录片《陈家冷》的摄影棚里，深情地回忆起恩师陆俨少对自己的教诲。

陈家冷当年考入杭州高级中学的第一个动念，就是因为杭州高级中学拥有李叔同、鲁迅、丰子恺、弘一法师、潘天寿等一大批名人大师学者。由于他的努力，终于有幸考入杭州高级中学，在以后的日子里，前辈学长便成了他做人学习的楷模。浙江省立第一师范学校（旧址位于今杭州高级中学），是中国建立最早的六大著名师范学校之一，前身是创建于1908年的浙江官立两级师范学堂。享有"北有京师学堂，南有浙江一师"的美誉。

1958年陈家冷考入浙江美术学院（如今的中国美术学院），当时潘天寿正是浙江美术学院的院长。陈家冷在浙江美术学院就读时，院长潘天寿的治学理念与中国画经典思想给了他深刻而长久的启发，这些理念和思想至今都深深记在他的脑海里，并作为他人生追求的最高奋斗目标。

2011年夏，纪录片《陈家泠》在杭州西湖正式开拍
In summer 2011, the documentary *Chen Jialing* started shooting officially in the West Lake, Hangzhou

Chen Jialing was born in Hangzhou in 1937 and graduated from Zhejiang Academy of Fine Arts in 1963. The West Lake was Chen Jialing's happiest childhood memory. Admitted first to The First Normal School of Zhejiang Province (today's Hangzhou High School), and then to Figure Painting Specialty of Chinese Department in Zhejiang Academy of Fine Arts (today's China Academy of Fine Arts), he transformed himself from an amateur to a professional artist. He often said: "My mother was my first art teacher, Dean Pan Tianshou was my soul teacher in artistic pursuit, and Lu Yanshao was my 'doctoral' supervisor." The art genes in his blood come from his native land, his mother and his alma mater. Hence it is most appropriate that the wide-screen color documentary *Chen Jialing* was shot in the West Lake, Hangzhou. In the film, Chen Jialing was sitting on a hand rowing boat decorated with blue calico. The girl rowing the boat was rocking her oar gently, and the boat was drifting on the smoky lake. Chen Jialing was mesmerized by the wonderland of the West Lake.

陈家泠 1937 年出生于杭州，1963 年毕业于浙江美术学院。西湖给儿时的他带来最快乐的记忆。从学徒进入学堂，考入杭州高级中学，后又考入浙江美术学院中国画系人物专业。他常说，母亲是他的启蒙老师，院长潘天寿是他艺术的灵魂导师，陆俨少是他的"博士生"导师。他人生中的艺术密码，就是来自"母土"，母亲与母校。所以，拍摄《陈家泠》彩色宽银幕纪录片选择在杭州西湖正式开拍是最恰当不过了。影片中陈家泠正坐在一艘装饰了蓝印花布的手划小船中，船娘悠悠地拨动着摇橹，小船悠悠在烟波漾漾的湖面中，而陈家泠却深深陶醉在这西湖梦幻的仙境之中。

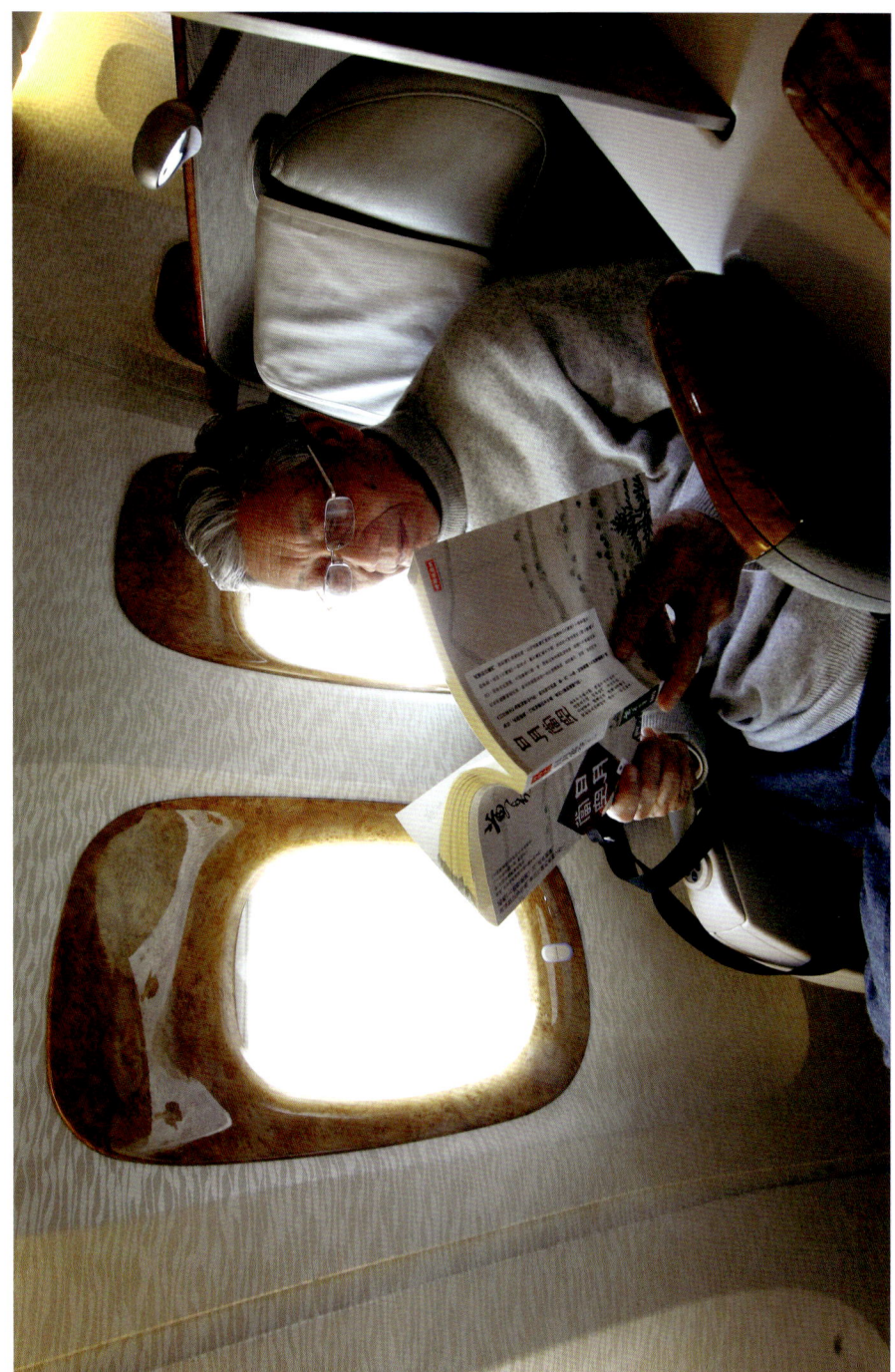

陈家泠出写生途中,在机舱里读书
Chen Jialing read in the cabin on his sketching trip

Every time Chen Jialing goes out for sketching, he makes a point to take three items along the way: a sketchbook, a camera and a martial arts novel. Reading martial arts novels is his favorite hobby, especially those written by Jin Yong such as *The Demi-Gods and Semi-Devils*, *The Legend of the Condor Heroes*, *The Deer and the Cauldron*, *The Legendary Swordsman*, *Chivalrous Couples of Apotheosis Eagles*, *Ode to Gallantry* and *The Heaven Sword and Dragon Saber*, etc. Whenever a new book is published, he will ask his friends at the publishing house to buy it as soon as possible. So literally he has read all of Jin Yong's martial arts novels from cover to cover and some over and over again. Especially on long-distance flights and high-speed trains, he would read for more than ten hours, and finish a thick novel on a round trip. Chen Jialing has another idiosyncrasy: He would synthesize what he has read or watched and form a set of his own art theory which not only embodies his artistic innovation but also realizes his theoretical innovation.

In order to know the actual situation of the old industrial zone in Shanghai, Chen Jialing took a field trip to the old factory zone with old factory buildings and rusty old equipment. He even ascended the rundown stairs, and commented with a tinge of regret: These are very rare "installation art pieces".

陈家泠登上锈迹斑斑的老旧厂房楼梯
Chen Jialing ascended the stairs of the rusty old factory building

陈家泠每次外出创作写生，途中必带三件物品：速写本、照相机、武侠小说。读武侠小说是他生活中的一大爱好，尤其是金庸的武侠小说。如《天龙八部》《射雕英雄传》《鹿鼎记》《笑傲江湖》《神雕侠侣》《侠客行》《倚天屠龙记》等。凡是新出版的，他都会第一时间托出版社的朋友买到手。可以讲金庸出版的所有武侠小说，他都仔细地认真反复看上好几遍，有些甚至要反复看上好几遍。陈家泠还有一个特点，无论看书、看电视机会融会贯通，一个往返的旅程，他就能看完一本厚厚的武侠小说，尤其在长途的飞机、高铁上，他会看书十几个小时，形成一套自己独特的艺术理论，这既体现了他的艺术创新，也实现了他的理论创新。

为了解上海老工业区的实况，陈家泠对老厂房和锈迹斑斑的老设备进行实地考察，甚至攀登破旧楼梯。对此，他不无感慨地说："这些都是非常难得的'装置艺术'。"

陈家泠为书法展创作
Chen Jialing created artworks for the calligraphy exhibition

In 2015, while climbing a height for painting, Chen Jialing accidentally fell and caused a femur fracture. After the operation, he checked into the International Guidu Hotel in Shanghai. In his second year at the hotel, he held his first calligraphy exhibition.

2015年，陈家泠因画画卷过高时，不小心摔倒，造成股骨骨折，手术出院后便入住上海国际贵都大饭店。入住酒店的第二年，他在酒店举办了生平第一个书法观摩展。

陈家泠在广东美术馆为热爱美术的小朋友上美术辅导课
Chen Jialing gave art tutorial classes to children who love art at Guangdong Art Museum

In Dec. 2009, Chen Jialing held a large-scale "Free Roaming" — Exhibition of Jialing's Artworks at Guangdong Art Museum. During the exhibition, he gave special art tutoring classes to the children who love art.

In Sep.2013, during his large-scale solo art exhibition *Sublimity* at the National Museum of China, Chen Jialing gave a lecture to the students of an art workshop at the invitation of Peking University. As a senior professor, Chen Jialing never requested any fee for lecturing at any school. If the school insisted on giving, he would donate the money, signing "Donated by Chen Jialing" on the envelope of lecture fees, and this lecture at Peking University was no exception.

陈家泠讲演时的情景和不同手势与讲课费捐献信封上签名合成的一组照片
A group of photos of Chen Jialing when he was speaking and gesturing during a lecture, and signing on the donation envelope of lecture fees

2009年12月，陈家泠在广东美术馆举办大型"神游——陈家泠作品展"。展览期间，他专门为热爱美术的少年儿童上美术辅导课。

2013年9月，陈家泠在中国国家博物馆举办大型个人艺术展"化境"期间，应北京大学邀请，为艺术研修班的学员讲课。陈家泠作为一名老教授在任何学校讲课都不收讲课费，如果学校一定要给那么他就会在讲课费的信封上写上"陈家泠捐赠"的字样进行捐赠，所以在这次北京大学的讲课也不例外。

2010年1月6日，陈家泠以矫健的动作攀登广东红砖厂的巨型水塔
On Jan.6, 2010, Chen Jialing ascended the giant water tower of Guangdong Red Brick Factory with vigorous movements

I have been a student of Chen Jialing for more than half a century (since 1970). For the past twenty years, I have accompanied, recorded and publicized him more like a friend and family. I have chronicled Chen Jialing's artistic career and detailed with my pen and camera how he explored every cave, climbed every mountain and reached every peak. With substantial data, I have exemplified his duty-bound, head-on and martyr-like pursuit of art.

This shot was taken when Chen Jialing was walking along a path in the mountainous area of Libo County, Guizhou Province. The low, narrow passageway forced everyone to bend their heads to get through. On the rock walls is the sign which reads "Sometimes a bow is necessary". It is a friendly reminder, but contains an element of philosophical truth.

陈家泠在贵州荔波山区低头弯腰路过小路
Chen Jialing bent over his body while walking along the path in the mountainous area of Libo County, Guizhou Province

做陈家泠学生已半个多世纪（1970年至今），陪伴陈家泠、记录陈家泠20年，是师生兼友人如家人。我完整地记录了陈家泠一路走来的艺术创作生涯，用全方位的数据详细地记载了陈家泠逢洞必钻、逢山必登、逢峰必攀的足迹，对他"义无反顾，一路前行，殉道般精神"的艺术人生做了全方位的探索。

这是陈家泠在贵州荔波山区路过一条小路的一个镜头，又低又窄的过道让每一个路过的人都不得不低头弯腰才能通过。在山岩的石壁上就有了"有时候，鞠躬也是一件必要的事"这块牌子。虽然是一块友情提醒的路牌，却有几分哲理。

陈家泠在九华山写生
Chen Jialing sketched On Mount Jiuhua

In preparation for the large-scale exhibition "Free Roaming in China's Famous Mountains" — An Exhibition of Chen Jialing's Artworks to be held at Anhui Provincial Museum in early spring 2011, Chen Jialing visited 12 mountains in China between 2010 and 2011, namely, Mount Huangshan in Anhui Province, Mount Lushan in Jiangxi Province, Mount Yandang in Zhejiang Province, five sacred mountains in China (Mount Taishan in the east of China, Mount Huashan in the west, Mount Hengshan in the south, Mount Songshan in the center, and Mount Henshan in the north), Mount Wutai in Shanxi Province, Mount Putuo in Zhejiang Province, Mount E'mei in Sichuan Province and Mount Jiuhua in Anhui Province. He considered himself "a wild animal", someone belonging to the wild nature. At the age of 74, he was still as physically agile when choosing an optimal shooting angle and as spiritually passionate when indulging in art life as he was 40 years ago. He enjoyed himself immensely visiting the scenic spots and places of cultural interest, because that is where his source of creation lies, and where "art is his password to life".

2011年初春，为在安徽省博物馆举办"神游——三山五岳四圣地"大展，陈家泠从2010年到2011年，他走遍了中国的三山五岳四圣地的12座大山，即黄山、庐山、雁荡山、东岳泰山、西岳华山、南岳衡山、中岳嵩山、北岳恒山与山西五台山、浙江普陀山、四川峨眉山、安徽九华山。虽然当时陈家泠已经74岁，但当年在山西五台山上选择角度的敏捷身影与对艺术生活充满无限激情的精神状态，可用陈家泠自己的话来形容："他是野生动物。"因为祖国大地、名山大川、乡村树林是他十分乐意去的地方，因为那里有他无限创作的源泉，"艺术是他的人生密码"。

陈家冷坐渔夫的竹筏在漓江上写生
Chen Jialing sketched on a fisherman's raft along Lijiang River

"世上无难事，只要肯登攀" 组照一
Group photo one: "Nothing is hard in this world if you dare to scale the heights"

Group photo "Nothing is hard in this world if you dare to scale the heights". This photo-shopped picture of the mountains and rivers Chen Jialing has walked through is a true portrayal of his life as an artist.

After visiting Chen Jialing's exhibition *Great Rivers and Gorgeous Mountains* in the National Museum of China and viewing the exquisite landscape works, a noted scholar remarked admiringly: "Mr. Chen Jialing is a master of Chinese painting. All the great rivers and mountains of China are in his heart. He has walked through them one by one and has manifested his patriotism with his artistic creation." These succinct words are a high appraisal of Chen Jialing's painting. In Chen Jialing's own words, he "runs", "paints" and "fights" to "portray the magnificent scenery of China, my motherland, which is the driving force for my pursuit of beauty and the powerhouse of my creation." In 1963, he was assigned to work in Shanghai after graduating from Zhejiang Academy of Fine Arts (today's China Academy of Art). In the span of 60 years, he has painted a wide range of sceneries, both domestic and international, from "Landscapes in the hometown" to "Landscapes of Li River in Guangxi", from "Famous Chinese mountains" to "Buddhist holy mountains", from "Magnificent motherland" to "Revolutionary sites", from "The Tibetan plateau" to "Beautiful Xinjiang", and from "The Treasure Island of Taiwan" to world-famous mountains and rivers. At the age of 86, he still takes his sketchbook and camera with him whenever he goes out.

"世上无难事，只要肯登攀"组照二
Group photo Two:"Nothing is hard in this world if you dare to scale the heights"

"世上无难事，只要肯登攀"组照。这是经过PS的一张陈家泠所走过的山山水水，是他艺术生涯的真实写照。

曾有一位哲人参观了陈家泠在中国国家博物馆"万水千山"厅里的一幅幅精美山水作品后，非常感慨地说："陈家泠先生是我国的国画大师，祖国的大好河山都装在他心里，他走过了祖国的山山水水，他是用艺术爱国。"短短数语，道出了陈家泠绘画精神的高度评价。用陈家泠自己的话说，就是三个字，即："跑"、"画"、"拼"。"祖国这么壮美的山河，是我追求美的动力与创作的源泉"。1963年，陈家泠从浙江美术学院毕业后被分到上海，整整第60个年头，他从"家乡山水"画到"广西漓江山水"，从"三山五岳"画到"佛教圣地山水"，从"青藏高原"画到"大美新疆"，从"祖国宝岛"画到世界名山大川，如今86岁的他每次外出，仍坚持带上写生本和照相机。

陈家泠在黄山飞来石写生
Chen Jialing sketched on Feilai Stone of Mount Huangshan

In 2021 and 2022, Chen Jialing held "The Red Star Shines over Me" — Calligraphy and Painting Exhibition of Revolutionary Sites and "Scale the Heights" — Invited exhibition of Chen Jialing's Works Commemorating the Centenary of Shanghai University in Shanghai Jiao Tong University and Shanghai University respectively. This is a vivid portrayal and track record of his 60-year art life devoted to expressing patriotism through painting.

2021年和2022年,他分别在上海交通大学、上海大学举办了"红星照我行""红色革命圣地书画大展"和"音登攀——纪念上海大学建校100周年陈家泠艺术邀请特展",这是他60年来用绘画爱国的生动写照与人生记录。

陈家泠与毛泽东、朱德、刘少奇、周恩来、任弼时的后代在作品《延安晨曦》前合影

Chen Jialing took a group photo in front of his work *Dawn in Yan'an* with the offsprings of Mao Zedong, Zhu De, Liu Shaoqi, Zhou Enlai and Ren Bishi

In Sep. 2017, "Sublimity" — Exhibition of Chen Jialing's Artworks was held at the National Museum of China. During the exhibition, Chen Jialing took a group photo in front of his work *Dawn in Yan'an* with the offsprings of Mao Zedong, Zhu De, Liu Shaoqi, Zhou Enlai and Ren Bishi.

In Oct. 2014, the documentary *Chen Jialing* was shown at Rome International Film Festival in Italy.

In Nov. 2015, the documentary *Chen Jialing* was shown in Los Angeles International Film Festival in USA, Brisbane International Film Festival in Australia and Hawaii International Film Festival in USA, and won three distinctions for Best Documentary Award and Cultural Ambassador Title.

陈家泠、纪录片导演蒋樵柯与上海电影制片厂总经理徐杰出席电影节
Chen Jialing attended the film festival with Jia Zhangke, director of the documentary, and Xu Jie, general manager of Shanghai Film Studios

2017年9月，陈家泠在中国国家博物馆举办"化境——陈家泠艺术展"，展览期间，陈家泠与毛泽东、朱德、刘少奇、周恩来，任那时的后代在作品《延安晨曦》前合影。

2014年10月，纪录片《陈家泠》在意大利罗马国际电影节荣誉展映。

2015年11月，纪录片《陈家泠》分别在美国洛杉矶国际电影节、澳大利亚布里斯班国际电影节、夏威夷美国国际电影节展映，荣获三项最佳纪录片大奖与文化大使奖。

2011年初春,陈家泠来到峨眉山,为大觉禅寺挥毫,书写了"智"字
In early spring 2011, Chen Jialing came to Mount Emei and wrote the character "智 (Wisdom)" for Temple of Great Awakening

陈家泠向上海大学党委书记成旦红、上海中医药大学党委书记曹锡康介绍展览情况
Chen Jialing introduced the exhibition to Cheng Danhong, Party Secretary of Shanghai University and Cao Xikang, Party Secretary of Shanghai University of Traditional Chinese medicine

"Traditional Chinese Medicine Joining Hands with Traditional Chinese Painting for the Benefit of Mankind"— exhibition of Chen Jialing's calligraphy and painting works on Chinese herbal medicine and "Compendium of Materia Medica" opened at Shanghai Museum of Traditional Chinese Medicine on Mar.8, 2024. Sponsored by Shanghai University and Shanghai University of Traditional Chinese Medicine, and organized by College of Continuing Education Shanghai University and Shanghai Museum of Traditional Chinese Medicine, it was a dialogue between traditional Chinese medicine and the art of painting and calligraphy spanning a thousand years.

"岐黄丹青 造福人类"——陈家泠中草药艺术书画与《本草纲目》展现场
Scene of "Traditional Chinese Medicine Joining Hands with Traditional Chinese Painting for the Benefit of Mankind" — exhibition of Chen Jialing's calligraphy and painting works on Chinese herbal medicine and "Compendium of Materia Medica"

一场跨越千年的中医药与书画艺术的对话，2024年3月8日，由上海大学、上海中医药大学主办，上海大学继续教育学院、上海中医药博物馆承办的"岐黄丹青 造福人类"——陈家泠中草药艺术书画与《本草纲目》展在上海中医药博物馆开幕。

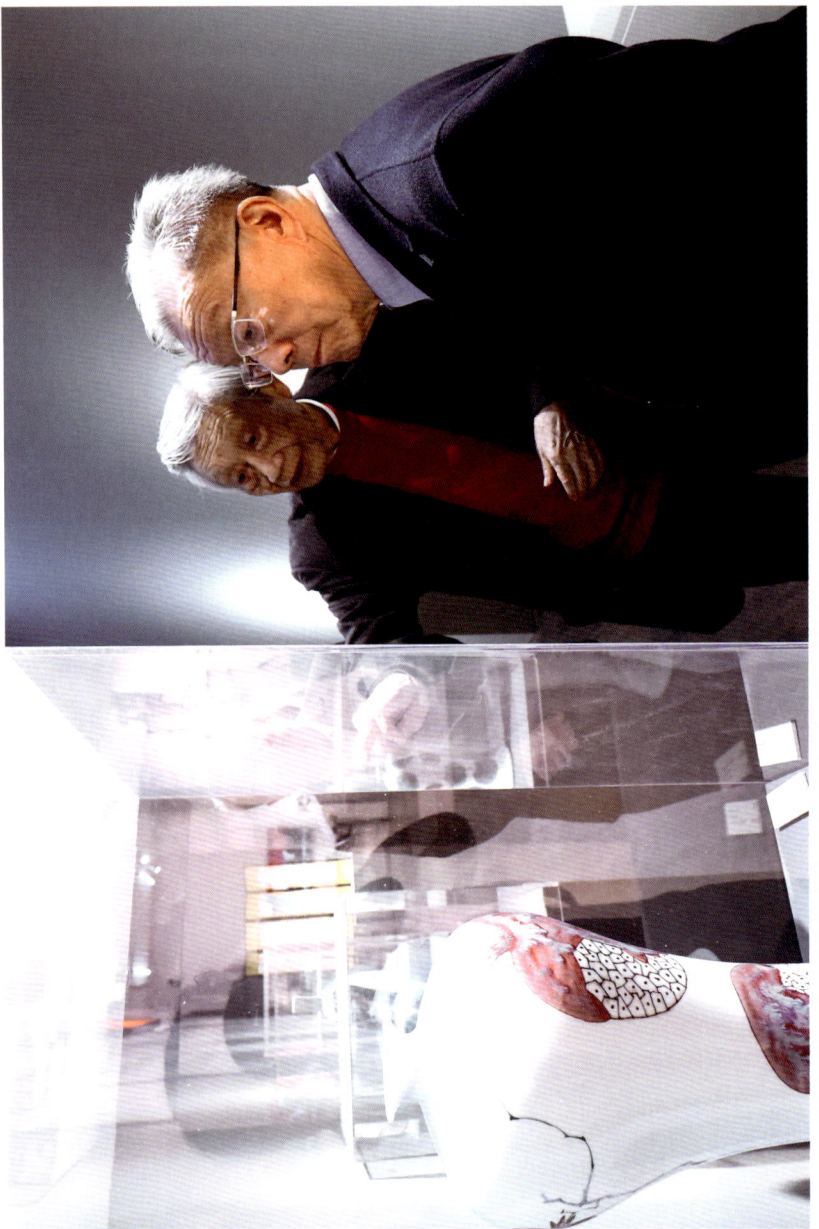

陈家泠陪同中医国大师施杞参观他在观缘的艺术工作室并进行深入地交流。
Chen Jialing accompanied Shi Qi, a master of traditional Chinese medicine, to visit his art studio at Guanyuan estate and exchanged views.

陈家泠与中医国大师施杞讨论中医药与中国书画的美学与哲学等的相互关系

Chen Jialing and Shi Qi, a master of traditional Chinese medicine, discussed the relationship of aesthetics and philosophy between traditional Chinese medicine and Chinese painting and calligraphy

巴黎科德利埃修道院艺术空间
The art space of Cordillere Monastery in Paris

"水岸丹青"陈家泠艺术展每天都接待大量的法国观众
"Chinese Painting on the Banks of Seine"--Chen Jialing's art exhibition received a large number of French visitors every day

On Apr.5, 2024, eve of the 60th anniversary of Sino-French diplomacy, the year of Sino-French cultural tourism and the opening ceremony of the Olympic Games in Paris, France, Chen Jialing held the art exhibition of "Chinese Painting on the Banks of Seine" at the art space of Cordillere Monastery in Paris.

2024年4月5日，陈家泠在中法建交60周年、中法文化旅游年以及法国巴黎奥运会开幕式前夕，在巴黎科德利埃修道院艺术空间举办"水岸丹青"陈家泠艺术展。

陈家泠在法国巴黎科德利埃修道院艺术空间举办"水岸丹青"陈家泠艺术展场景
Scene of Chen Jialing's art exhibition — "Chinese Painting on the Banks of Seine" at the art space of Cordillere Monastery in Paris

陈家泠在展览开幕式上发言
Chen Jialing spoke at the opening ceremony of the exhibition

展览期间还举办各种形式的文化活动
Various cultural activities were also held during the exhibition

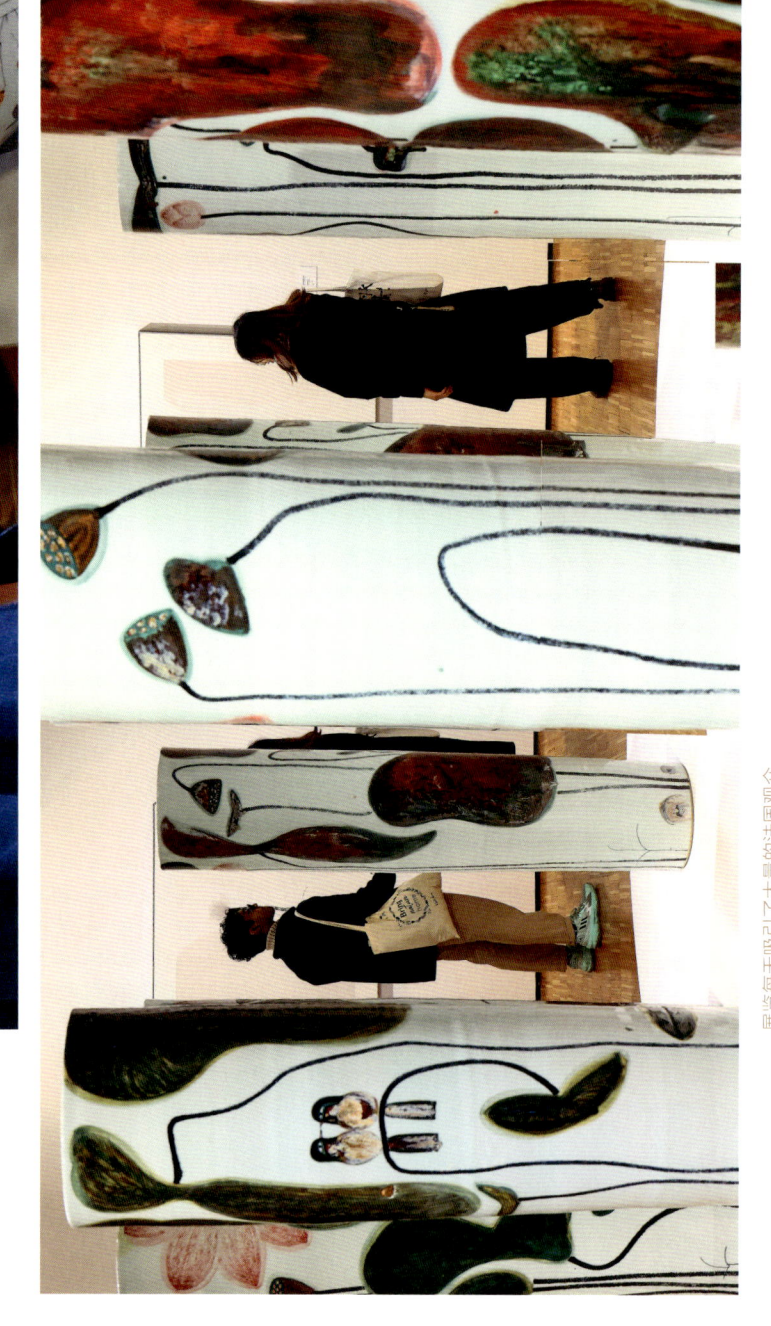

展览每天吸引了大量的法国观众
The exhibition received a large number of French visitors every day

为了支持"水岸丹青"陈家泠艺术展,非遗缂丝织造的陈家泠作品《荷花》进行中
To support Chen Jialing's art exhibition—"Chinese Painting on the Banks of Seine", *Lotus*, a piece of Chen Jialing's works made from silk, an intangible cultural heritage, was in progress

为了运送展览的作品，义乌中欧班列专门开辟了新义欧巴黎专列

In order to transport the exhibits, the Chinese-Europe train in Yiwu set up a special train from Yiwu, China to Paris, Europe

陈家泠为展览创作《南屏晚钟》

Chen Jialing worked on "Nanping Evening Bell" for the exhibition

2023年12月13日,陈家泠江西景德镇望龙瓷厂
On Dec.13, 2023, Chen Jialing painted at Wanglong porcelain factory in Jingdezhen, Jiangxi Province

2011年12月,在上海电影制片厂摄影棚拍摄纪录片《陈家泠》的一张剧照
A still taken during the filming of the documentary *Chen Jialing* at the studio of Shanghai Film Studios in Dec 2011

Epilogue

"Scale the Heights" is an exhibition of my photographical works to celebrate the centennial anniversary of Shanghai University. It is a track record I have kept of Chen Jialing's art life for many years.

With multiple angles, multiple forms and multiple dimensions, the collection of works embodies the dramatic art life of Chen Jialing and his unflinching spirit of martyrdom from a unique perspective. The works reflect his perseverance in pursuing innovation and exploration on the road of art. They embody his love of nature and his thoughts on life and society, they showcase his keen observation and rich imagination, and his responsibility for and commitment to contemporary art and modern life. Through this album, I hope more people can gain insights into Chen Jialing's views on art, life and the world, as well as the stories and achievements of "scaling the heights" behind these photographs. This is also a calling to SHUers to carry forward the spirit of the times.

This photography exhibition held at the centenary of Shanghai University means a lot to me. Not only is it a summary and review of my photographing career, but also a high tribute to my alma mater. This album is the result of my 20-odd years of unremitting efforts and persistence in systematic creation. Using my camera, I hope to fully reproduce Chen Jialing's artistic life and the creative process in the portrayal of light and shadow, natural landscapes, harmony between man and nature, etc.

In the process of editing and publishing the album, I have been most fortunate and privileged to receive so much support and guidance from the leaders of Shanghai University, and from the leaders and teachers of

后 记

"肯登攀"是我在上海大学百年校庆之际举办的摄影展主题名，也是我多年来拍摄记录陈家泠人生的艺术轨迹的写照。

本书中的作品以多种角度、多样形式，多面人生魅力和多维创造力的独特视角，表现了陈家泠先生的多彩艺术人生与义无反顾的殉道精神。作品反映了他在艺术道路上不断追求创新和勇于探索的毅力；反映了他对自然的热爱和对生活与社会的思考；展现了他敏锐的观察力和丰富的想象力；展示了他对当代艺术及时代责任的担当。通过这本画册，希望能够向更多的人展示陈家泠的艺术观、人生观、世界观；让更多人了解他的摄影背后"肯登攀"的故事与成就；也是弘扬上大精神的一种时代感召。

百年校庆时刻，我举办的这场名为"肯登攀"陈家泠艺术足迹摄影作品展，对我而言意义非凡。它不仅是我摄影生涯的一个总结和回顾，也是用摄影展的形式，向母校致以的崇高敬意。这本画册是我20多年来不懈努力与坚持系统创作的成果，旨在通过镜头，完整地再现陈家泠的艺术人生、奋斗的形象，创作历程，是一本集光影艺术、山河风貌、人与自然等的交响。

在画册的编辑出版过程中，得到了上海大学领导的高度重视与大力支持，得到了上海大学继续教育学院、上海美术学院、上

College of Continuing Education Shanghai University, Shanghai Academy of Fine Arts and Shanghai University Press. I would particularly like to thank my wife Jiang Huizheng for her understanding and devotion all these years. Besides, my family and friends have given me strength and courage when I need it most. I gratefully acknowledge all your care and encouragement.

I hope that through this beautifully-produced album, readers can be inspired by the spirit of "scaling the heights" characteristic of the times and the school spirit of Shanghai University of "The Unity of Knowledge and Action, the Pursuit of Excellence" advocated while appreciating the beauty and countless moving stories behind the pictures. Let's join hands to write a more brilliant new chapter in the course of our career and life.

Xu Genshun

海大学出版社的领导与老师们的鼎力协助,特别是得到了我的爱人姜慧珍几十年如一日默默无闻的理解与支持。此外,我还要感谢毛时安老师和我的亲朋好友,是他们在我最需要的时候给了我力量和坚持的勇气。

希望通过这本精彩的画册,各位在欣赏美与背后无数感人故事的同时,让"肯登攀"的时代精神与"知行合一,追求卓越"的上大校风,共同促进各位在追求事业的人生旅途中谱写更加辉煌的新篇章!

许根顺

A brief introduction to the author

Born in Jan.1949 in Shanghai. Graduated from Shanghai Art School in 1970, taught at Shanghai University of Engineering Sciences in 1978, graduated from Central Academy of Art and Design in 1983, graduated from Department of Journalism in Jiangxi University. Served as office manager of Xinjinjiang Hotel and office manager of Xinjinjiang Company Limited in 1988. Guest professor at School of Continuing Education, Shanghai University since Apr.2023. Guest professor at Shanghai Museum of Traditional Chinese medicine since Jan. 2014. Member of Shanghai Public Diplomacy Association, member of China Photographers Association, member of China Popular Color Society, member of International Chinese photographic Federation. Won Shanghai Award for Outstanding Photography in 1984-1985, over 60 photographs have won gold, silver and bronze awards in international and Chinese Photography Grand Prix.

Took part in the photography work of a series of major foreign affairs activities including Shanghai APEC Conference in 2001, Shanghai Cooperation Organization Summit and The Eleventh International Council for Action in 2006, Shanghai World Expo in 2010 and CICA Summit in 2014. Took documentary photos for the heads of government, dignitaries, leaders of international organizations and first ladies of 180 countries such as the United States, Russia, Britain, France, Germany, and Japan. Collect nearly 600 first-day covers of China's reform and opening-up signed by heads of state and heads of government from around the world.

Published *State Guests in Shanghai*, by Xu Genshun , Shanghai Pictorials Publishing House, 2008. *First Ladies in Shanghai*, by Jiao Yang and Xu Genshun, Shanghai Pictorials Publishing House, 2010. *The Art of Chen Jialing*, Anhui Fine Arts Publishing House, 2018, editor-in-chief, Wang Chunfa, curatorial and design editor, Xu Genshun. *Footprints of Shanghai Fine Arts School — Chen Jialing*, edited by Xu GenshJn, Shanghai University Press, 2019. *Red Star Shines over Me: Chen Jialing's Artworks of Revolutionary Sites*, deputy editor-in-chief and video producer, Xu Genshun, Shanghai Literature and Art Publishing House, 2021.

许根顺简介

1949年1月生于上海。1970年毕业于上海美术学校，1978年任上海工程技术大学教师，1983年毕业于中央工艺美术学院，1984年毕业于江西大学新闻系。1988年任上海锦江大酒店办公室主任、股份有限公司办公室主任。2023年4月，任上海大学继续教育学院特聘教授；2024年1月，受聘上海中医药博物馆客座教授。为上海公共外交协会会员、中国摄影家协会会员、中国流行色学会会员、世界华人摄影协会会员。曾获1984—1985上海优秀摄影家奖，60余幅摄影作品分别获国际、中国各地摄影大奖美金、银、铜奖。

参加2001年上海APEC会议、2006年上合六国峰会、第11届国际行动理事会、2010年上海世博会和2014年亚信峰会等一系列重大外事活动的摄影工作。为美国、俄罗斯、英国、法国、德国、日本等近180个国家的政府首脑、政界要员、国际组织领导人以及第一夫人的拍摄纪实照片。收藏有世界各国元首、政府首脑签名的近600封中国改革开放的首日封。

出版有《国宾在上海》，许根顺摄，上海锦绣文章出版社2008年版；《第一夫人在上海》，焦扬主编，许根顺摄影，上海锦绣文章出版社2010年版；《陈家泠艺术》，安徽美术出版社2018年版，主编王春法、张子龙，许根顺装帧设计；《上海足迹——陈家泠》，许根顺主编，上海大学出版社2019年版；《红星照我行：陈家泠革命圣地作品》，许根顺任副主编、影像摄制，上海文艺出版社2021年版。

图书在版编目（CIP）数据

肯登攀：陈家泠天马行空艺术人生 / 许根顺摄影、撰文. -- 上海：上海大学出版社，2024.9. -- ISBN 978-7-5671-5054-6

Ⅰ. K825.72

中国国家版本馆 CIP 数据核字第 20247KY322 号

策划统筹	邓 江　周丽昀　严惠珏　王惠珏 房 林　黄 欢　戴骏豪　傅玉芳
策划编辑	上海大学继续教育学院 "公共外交与城市文化"许根顺工作室
特别鸣谢	中国银行上海分行
责任编辑	柯国富　邹亚楠
技术编辑	金 鑫　钱宇坤
英文翻译	李 欣
整体设计	上海袁银昌平面设计工作室　袁银昌　李 静

书　　名	肯登攀——陈家泠天马行空艺术人生
摄影　撰文	许根顺
出版发行	上海大学出版社
社　　址	上海市上大路 99 号
邮政编码	200444
网　　址	https://www.shupress.cn
发行热线	021-66135112
出 版 人	戴骏豪
印　　刷	上海雅昌艺术印刷有限公司
经　　销	各地新华书店
开　　本	787mm×1092mm 1/8
印　　张	42.5
字　　数	850 千字
版　　次	2024 年 9 月第 1 版
印　　次	2024 年 9 月第 1 次
书　　号	ISBN 978-7-5671-5054-6/K·292
定　　价	800.00 元